D1463534

YOU CAN

Use an interactive WHITE BOARD

Consultant Editor:
Julie Cogill

FOR AGES
7-11

"There is a
whiteboard revolution
in UK schools"
Primary National Strategy

Consultant Editor
Julie Cogill

Illustrations
Mike Phillips

Authors
Jon Audain
Julie Cogill
Anthony David
Martin Flute
Sara Fielder

Series Designer
Catherine Mason

Designer
Melissa Leeke

Additional Authors
Anne Cooper
Heather Cromie
Karen Mawer

Editor
Frances Ridley

Assistant Editor
Niamh O'Carroll

Cover concept/designer
Anna Oliwa

Cover illustration
© bananastock/punchstock;
SMART Board Interactive Whiteboard © SMART Technologies Inc

Text © 2006 Jon Audain, Julie Cogill,
Anthony David, Martin Flute,
Sara Fielder.

© 2006 Scholastic Ltd

Designed using Adobe InDesign

Published by Scholastic Ltd
Villiers House
Clarendon Avenue
Leamington Spa
Warwickshire CV32 5PR

www.scholastic.co.uk

Printed by Bell and Bain Ltd.
4 5 6 7 8 9   7 8 9 0 1 2 3 4 5

British Library Cataloguing-in-Publication Data
A catalogue record for this book is available from the British Library.
ISBN 0-439-96540-3
ISBN 978-0439-96540-8

The rights of the authors have been asserted in accordance with the Copyright, Designs and
Patents Act 1988.

Contents

Contents

Introduction

What is an interactive whiteboard?

'Every class should have one!'

This comment about interactive whiteboards has been made by many teachers who have used them across the primary age groups. Many teachers believe that the interactive whiteboard is an important modern development that will bring about change in teaching and learning in the primary school.

The interactive whiteboard is attached to a computer so that images can be clearly projected on to the screen or whiteboard. It is different from using a projector because the board itself is sensitive to touch and operates as an interactive device. When the board is activated, and then touched with a finger or a special pen, it responds in exactly the same way as a computer screen responds to the manipulation of a mouse.

About this book

The 50 ideas presented in this book are about teaching and learning with an interactive whiteboard, and about how you can use ICT to create inspiring lessons. One question that often arises is whether using an interactive whiteboard is about teaching, learning or using ICT. The answer is that it's about all three. The interactive whiteboard will not do the teaching for you but it will give you access to many more resources – audio, video, images, websites and interactive activities – that were previously unavailable for the whole class to view, discuss, interact with and learn from.

The following comments were made by teachers who had used interactive whiteboards for one year:

'Everything is big and bright on the screen, so that the whole class can see text and images clearly. I can annotate images in response to the children's comments and bring them up on the board the next day to remind them about what we discussed.'
(Year 6 teacher)

'It's just the vast number of different things that you can put in front of the children to enhance their learning. Teaching and learning are obviously not just about the whiteboard, but with the whiteboard you can do so much more.'
(Year 4 teacher)

'It is refreshing and innovative for teachers to be able to experiment with new ways of presenting information. It gives you great inspiration, as a teacher, to look at things in a different and exciting new way.'
(Year 5 teacher)

'It just brings content to life: it's such a time-saver and there are so many resources available that it makes lessons inspiring.'
(Year 3 teacher)

Whiteboards and teaching

At a basic level, the interactive whiteboard can be used as a chalkboard. Although this is not necessarily the best use of the available technology, the whiteboard does have many advantages over a traditional chalkboard in that multiple pages can be created. Work displayed at the beginning of a lesson can therefore be accessed at any time, with just the click of a button, if teachers want to review earlier teaching points. All the pages can be displayed or reviewed in sequence for ease of navigation. Other useful features include the ability to change colour instantly, and the availability of simple templates for tables or grids to help in organising points made in whole-class work. Using the whiteboard in this way will help new users to develop confidence and we hope that this book will also be a useful tool to get you started on your adventure into new ways of teaching and learning.

Whiteboards and learning

If you already have some experience in using the whiteboard, however, then we hope the teaching suggestions will take you further. What is especially important is the facility the whiteboard provides to share children's learning experiences. This does not mean just asking individual children to come to the board to suggest answers, but using the facilities of the board to display and discuss ideas so that everyone can share in the learning experience. The whiteboard also allows teachers to explore and relate the thinking of individuals to the context of the learning that is happening in the class as a whole. In the best whiteboard classrooms, teachers comment that sometimes they can stand aside while children themselves 'lead' the lesson by presenting their ideas to the class for further discussion.

Whiteboards and ICT

This book is not intended to teach ICT skills but it does provide ideas for how ICT can be used to create classroom resources for the whiteboard. There are particular hints on how you can use Microsoft Word, PowerPoint, Excel and resources found on the Internet to make lessons more interesting.

We hope you will add to the ideas presented in this book by using the photocopiable templates provided at the back of the book to record your own uses of the whiteboard. Last but not least, it is important to share both your whiteboard skills and ideas for teaching and learning with colleagues. Sharing skills and resources in this way will not only save you a great deal of time, but will also help to create a collaborative teaching community and enhance the learning experiences of children.

You Can... **Use an interactive whiteboard to prepare lessons**

One of the advantages of using a whiteboard is that content, slides and flipcharts can be prepared away from the classroom in advance. A whiteboard provides you with the opportunity to give high quality presentations, and to use a wide range of resources. Lessons can be planned and content loaded onto the board at appropriate times during the day, thereby leaving more time for teaching and learning!

Thinking points

● The design of your presentation should not take precedence over its content.

● Make sure the resources you use provide appropriate content and presentation for the age group you are teaching.

● Think about the questions you use as you prepare flipcharts or slide shows. Use open, rather than closed, questions that draw on children's knowledge.

● Consider how children can engage in an interactive way. Is there potential for children to demonstrate what they can do at the board? Does the activity lend itself to a collaborative task, such as whole-class creative writing? (A photocopiable sheet has been provided on page 61 to help plan your whiteboard tasks.)

● Consider planning a programme of learning in advance, for example across three lessons, so that continuity and progression can be built in.

Tips, ideas and activities

● Be flexible! Pre-prepared slides or flipchart pages are useful but be prepared to take the lead from what children are learning and how the lesson develops. You don't have to stick to your 'script'.

● Keep an organised electronic file of all lessons, so that you can recall and adapt a lesson for a different learning experience. A file of hard-copy lessons is also useful for quick access. If children need to recap their existing knowledge, use the files to check how the topic was originally taught and review appropriate pages before moving to new work.

● Build up a range of illustrations, demonstrations and visual aids (subject to copyright restrictions) to help retain children's attention and motivation and develop their understanding.

● When you are searching for resources, make a note of images, websites or video resources (copyright permitting) that may be useful for particular subjects , even if the resource is not immediately relevant. Many a frustrating hour can be spent looking for that 'perfect' image you saw early last week!

● Remember that children need to engage in their own learning and work independently for part of the lesson. Three slides and an illustration, together with questions, answers and discussion, can take a substantial slice of lesson time.

You Can... Use an interactive whiteboard to show websites

The use of websites can add much to a lesson, be it map-making skills or writing biographies. The interactive whiteboard is an obvious and excellent tool for displaying and navigating through the wealth of resources that can be found on the World Wide Web (www). There are literally millions of websites to choose from. Using a search engine, which is basically an index to a large number of websites, will help you to find what you want.

Thinking points

● If a website meets the needs of your objective then use it – it does not pay to spend hours looking for that perfect site!

● Using educational search engines such as the National Grid for Learning (www.ngfl.gov.uk) will reduce the amount of time you spend searching for appropriate content.

● Visit the site to check its suitability before using it with the whole class. Ask yourself:

   1) Is the language accessible?

   2) Is the font large enough?

   3) Does the content of the site support your lesson objectives?

   4) Can the children clearly see the text or images on the whiteboard? Do you need to modify the background?

● A firewall filters for keywords on a site and prevents the user from entering inappropriate sites by mistake. If your school has a firewall it is possible that a website you can access at home may not be available in school.

Tips, ideas and activities

● Use websites on the whiteboard to give children global experiences, for sources of evidence in history and to find out about the background of an author or literary text.

● Text and pictures can be copied from many websites by highlighting them (clicking and dragging the cursor over the desired area), copying them (Ctrl + C) and then pasting them (Ctrl + V) into a word processing document or on to an interactive whiteboard flipchart.

● Use the Favourites button, found on the Internet Task Bar, to store your favourite websites. By doing this, you will be able to return to websites more easily, particularly if you are in a hurry!

● As you load a website, explain to children the processes that you are using and which buttons you are clicking on with your pen or finger. This has obvious benefits for the children's ICT skills and you will quickly find that the children start to point out any errors that you make.

● If children have computer access ask them to continue their Internet research at home. (NB Make sure that you have checked and approved a website before recommending it to the children for secondary research at home.)

You Can... **Use an interactive whiteboard to show video resources**

Video material offers a range of unique experiences that can transport children to worlds they might never otherwise experience. An interactive whiteboard enables video resources to be accessed efficiently. It allows you to integrate video much more easily within a lesson, without the need to move children or television monitors. The way you access film resources will depend on what equipment is available to you. Film resources may be accessed via a video recorder, a DVD, a CD-ROM, or downloaded from the web or a local server. Without a very fast Internet connection, however, video streaming in a classroom is not advisable.

Thinking points

● Consider how the video links to the lesson and whether it will be used to introduce a topic, as a major resource in teaching a topic or to consolidate previous work.

● Think carefully about how much video to show. Since it is easy to access through the whiteboard, two or three minutes may be enough to illustrate a teaching point. On the other hand, 15 minutes may be required to give sufficient context to capture children's engagement and interest and to provide real learning.

● Preview the resource to consider where the video might be paused, so that children can predict what might happen next or to find out what children have previously understood. Pausing the video helps to give a more interactive experience.

Tips, ideas and activities

● You can use video to:
  ● show the wider world, through films of natural phenomena, animals in habitat, volcanoes, distant and inaccessible places and points of view from different people
  ● show the historical world, through archive film, examples of oral history and the dramatisation of historical events
  ● show the scientific world, through slow motion or time lapse images and the use of magnified images through an electron microscope
  ● show the emotional or inner world, through the experiences of different people, using case studies or drama reconstructions to encourage empathy with someone else's situation
  ● show the world of literature, through dramatisations
  ● move from the concrete to the abstract in mathematics, through a split screen or through images that gradually transform
  ● create motivation in what is to be learned by the use of interesting case studies, animation, cartoons, humour and drama.

● After viewing, discuss with the children what the film sequence was about to help consolidate their learning.

● Most importantly, if the video sequence uses humour or lends itself to joining in, encourage children to do this and enjoy it with them as a whole class activity.

You Can... Use an interactive whiteboard for children's presentations

Many children enjoy showing and demonstrating their work in front of the class. Using the whiteboard, children's work can be displayed on a large screen so everyone can share and discuss it. Using programs such as PowerPoint helps children to structure their work and produce professional presentations regardless of their level of attainment. Less confident learners in particular can succeed when using the computer – particularly those who struggle with written work. The computer will assist children in improving the presentation of their work and help their self-esteem.

Thinking points
● Consider whether the children are familiar with the main functions of the presentation software. For example, will they be able to plan the types of slide they will need to use? Do they know how to change fonts and type sizes? Can they add prepared animations?

● Consider asking pairs of children to share a presentation. The whiteboard can be a great vehicle for promoting collaborative learning.

● Consider which activities may be appropriate for children's presentations, for example:

  ● a presentation to the whole class by a small group demonstrating the research they have undertaken on a particular issue

  ● a presentation by the class at assembly, to the whole school

  ● an account of a school visit by the class, for a parents evening.

● Think of different ways in which children can share their work with parents and other carers.

Tips, ideas and activities
● If children working in small groups are asked to provide a class presentation on an issue, encourage them to choose one in which they will want to participate, for example animal welfare.

● Discuss with children the conventions of writing for presentations, for example the need for clear and succinct text on each slide.

● Encourage the children to plan how they might find images for their presentations, for example Clip Art, the Internet (copyright permitting), or digital photographs.

● Encourage children to look for pictures that enhance the information in their presentations, and that are not just decorative.

● Explain that slides will help the children to make their presentation look professional but that the clarity and content of each slide is more important than its design.

● When presenting, many children might be tempted to just read out the contents of each slide. To begin with, allow them to do this to gain confidence. In time, encourage them to add more detail to their presentations, using the slides as prompts rather than scripts.

● Give children the opportunity to practise their presentations, so that they are clear and confident about what they are going to say.

● After the big event, congratulate the children and celebrate their success.

You Can... **Use an interactive whiteboard for PowerPoint presentations**

One of the greatest strengths of using a whiteboard is that information can be presented clearly. Words and pictures can be combined in a variety of interesting and colourful ways. PowerPoint is a high-powered software tool designed to present text, charts, graphs, sound effects, video and animations in a dynamic slide show format. It is ideal for use on the interactive whiteboard. You can enhance your PowerPoint presentation by asking open-ended questions, to develop discussion work and draw a more personal response from the children.

Thinking points

● Think carefully about the pace of your presentation. Avoid using too many slides. Break up the presentation by adding in *Points to discuss*, or a small activity.

● When presented with a range of information, how many of us read the smaller print? Don't put too much text on each slide and make sure the font size is large enough.

● Remember; *A picture tells a thousand words*: using pictures in your PowerPoint presentations can save time, money and resources. When pictures are enlarged on a whiteboard the whole class can share the resource easily.

● Think about the design and impact of each slide. The human eye is drawn to information that is large, clearly presented and uncluttered. Effective adverts use pictures and large text to convey a message. The same theory can be applied to presentations relating to teaching and learning. Large, clearly presented text and relevant, eye-catching pictures will be easier to understand.

Tips, ideas and activities

● Experiment by changing the background to your slides. A simple splash of colour or a pattern will liven up the screen. A cream background, rather than white, may be easier on the reader's eyes.

● Use effects sparingly. A presentation in which every sentence and picture is animated can be overbearing and leave the audience feeling pale and nauseous.

● Explore the use of the different Action Buttons. These buttons perform an action when pressed and offer a quick and easy way of linking pages together (this is known as hyperlinking). Below are examples of the different types of Action Buttons that can be inserted into a presentation:

● To insert an Action Button using PowerPoint:

> 1) Click on the Slide Show menu and then scroll down to Action Buttons.
>
> 2) A menu will appear displaying the different buttons that can be inserted into a presentation. By hovering the cursor over each button a label will appear, informing you of its function.
>
> 3) Click on the button required and a cross will appear.
>
> 4) Hold down the left-hand mouse button and drag the cross. Click where you want to position it and the Action Button will appear.

You Can... Use an interactive whiteboard for effective starters

The whiteboard offers a huge range of experiences to motivate visual, kinaesthetic and aural learning. Starter materials range from a few minutes of video and television footage, to websites, images from the software library or a blank board with the facility to write, draw, erase and save. An effective starter will highlight the context of what children will be learning by reflecting on previous learning. The whiteboard can help you to do this: for example, you could show a slide used in a previous lesson, but highlight new facts.

Thinking points

● Think about when the starter takes place. If children are coming into the classroom just before the lesson, display something that will grab their attention as they are settling down to work: a poem for the whole class to share, for example, or a simple number puzzle (*Which of these numbers are odd?* or *Which of these numbers are multiples of seven?*).

● Consider the timing of the starter. Avoid using complex resources or lengthy explanation.

● Vary the types of resources you use. If an image is over-used, its impact can be lost. Also, different resources will appeal and motivate different children.

● Consider the purpose of the starter and how the whiteboard might be used to highlight it. For example, the purpose might be to sharpen and rehearse skills, to identify facts which children should know by heart or to review work done at home.

Tips, ideas and activities

● Use thought bubbles to record children's knowledge. If appropriate, ask children to suggest categories into which their ideas can be sorted, so the information is more accessible. Ask children to drag and drop their ideas into their chosen categories.

● Save children's initial ideas and return to them in the plenary session. Make a note of any new knowledge taught or learned during the lesson.

● Show children a series of images, for example a set of buildings, and ask them to explain what they have in common and what is different.

● Use a set of images to stimulate creative writing. Ask children to come to the board, sequence the images and then describe their stories. In this way several different stories may emerge, depending on how the images are sequenced.

● Suggest a new topic to children and ask them how they could find facts about this topic at the start of the lesson. Demonstrate the use of an Internet search engine, such as www.google.co.uk, to find links to new information.

● Start with a ten-minute video, television show or DVD. Use this to prompt speaking and listening activities such as debate, discussion and role play.

You Can... **Use an interactive whiteboard for effective plenary sessions**

The plenary session allows the teacher and children to summarise and reflect upon the learning, and highlight and tackle any misconceptions. A whiteboard makes it easy to revisit the main teaching objective. Images and information can be quickly referred to, in the order in which they were taught, from any saved flipchart pages. If misconceptions have arisen, flipchart pages can be annotated with another colour and resaved for follow-up lessons. The activity could be remodelled with different images and used again to reinforce the learning, perhaps in a subsequent starter.

Thinking points

● Consider the timing of the plenary session. The lesson may be just before a break, when children are tired or have lost concentration. Children should be asked to remain focused for no more than ten minutes.

● Concentration often wanes during plenary sessions. Consider using different media, such as websites, games, television or video clips to reinforce concepts and refocus the children.

● Think about using different visual images from those used in the main part of the lesson to emphasise the learning objective, but explain them in the same way.

● Think about how you might refer back to saved flipchart pages to analyse the lesson and aid future planning.

● Consider the different purposes of a plenary session and how the whiteboard might be used to highlight these. For example, ask children to present or explain their work, draw together key learning points or make links to other work.

Tips, ideas and activities

● When children are feeding back, encourage them to illustrate what they have learned using the Pen function on a blank flipchart page. Children's writing is often small, so enlarge it for the whole class to see.

● If time is available, scan in some of the children's work, so that they can present and explain it to the whole class.

● Depending on what equipment is available, children can be filmed during the main part of the lesson, especially for a role play, drama or PE lesson. Use the video to recap and evaluate lesson activities during the plenary session.

● Compare and contrast a short video clip with that taught in the main part of the lesson. For example, if the main part of the lesson considered historical artefacts, use a clip showing those artefacts in use.

● Visit a website that is related to the lesson. For example, if the children have been looking at a painting, visit an art gallery website to show how a range of different artists have painted similar subjects.

● Following the principles of Assessment for Learning, use a package such as Excel to devise and enlarge a spreadsheet for children to self-monitor their understanding of the objectives. This can be used later to modify the lesson for use on another occasion.

You Can... **Use an interactive whiteboard for effective revision**

Any document or flipchart you have created can be saved on to the computer to create a bank of saved lessons that can be accessed at any time to revise a selected objective. This is particularly effective when revisiting learning objectives from earlier in a week and clarifying any misconceptions. If you are conducting more formal revision sessions, for example for the National Tests, the BBC website (www.bbc.co.uk/revision) offers plenty of models, guides and lesson ideas to help you and your class, both at home and in school.

Thinking points

● What is the purpose of the revision? Remember to keep the lesson succinct and to the point. It is important that the children review only past objectives. Ensure that new objectives do not creep in inadvertently.

● The whiteboard can help you to keep revision fresh. Consider different ways of presenting the topic, for example through video clips, websites and animations.

● Consider ways to involve the children with the revision session. The interactive whiteboard appeals to kinaesthetic and visual learners: involve these children in leading the session by showing previous work or demonstrating skills.

● Revisit previously-saved lesson ideas – particularly any children's work. Saved material will trigger past learning experiences and can be used to address any misconceptions.

● Remember to check copyright restrictions before using images from websites.

Tips, ideas and activities

● Use multiple-choice tests on the whiteboard. These can be easily prepared in PowerPoint using text and Action Buttons (see page 11). Check that all children can see the multiple choice options clearly, as the dropdown menus sometimes have very small text. Ask the whole class to look at the options for each question and to vote for the correct one. Alternatively, ask why the other options are incorrect. Questions are often cleverly constructed to draw out common misconceptions.

● Visit your whiteboard supplier's website. Such websites often offer a rich source of pre-prepared lessons that can be downloaded and used for revision.

● Visit the National Literacy and Numeracy sites. All of the transition and revision materials can be accessed and edited on screen, in the same way that you would edit any screen shot. This allows you to prepare enlarged, clean copies of the resources rather than relying on smaller, A3, black-and-white photocopies.

The camel walks 3500m in one morning.
The next day he walks twice as far.
How far has he walked altogether?

a. 10 500 metres ☐

b. 35 000 metres ☐

c. 7000 metres ☐

You Can... **Use an interactive whiteboard to share effective teaching**

The arrival of an interactive whiteboard often generates excitement, enthusiasm and anticipation among teaching staff. Actually using the whiteboard, however, can be a roller coaster experience. There are the highs when things go right and the full potential of the whiteboard is realised; and there are the lows when the technology fails to do what is wanted. It is important to share different experiences, in order to share effective practice and further teaching and learning.

Thinking points

● Think about who is available for help when whiteboard problems occur: for example, the ICT co-ordinator, another colleague or the most ICT-competent children in your class.

● Make sure that lines of communication with technical support are established and kept open.

● Changing ways of teaching is an exciting challenge and there are plenty of opportunities for change when using a whiteboard. Be optimistic when developing your skills, and experiment – after all, there's always the manual for back-up!

● Consider what the word 'effective' means in terms of teaching. (The dictionary defines it as *producing the desired effect*.) The most effective whiteboard activities are interactive. When planning, consider what the children could do at the whiteboard during the lesson. If you 'deliver' the lesson without involving them, the potential interactivity will be lost.

Tips, ideas and activities

● Don't use the whiteboard for every lesson. Produce materials targeted at one subject area that will actively engage the children.

● Consider 'team-teaching' to begin with. Try to:
  ● plan lessons with a colleague in the same year group if possible and share the preparation load
  ● arrange your planning meetings in the same room as the whiteboard, activities can then be tried out and discussed
  ● follow up your jointly planned lesson by considering how effective the lesson was for each class of children, and modifying appropriately
  ● keep a shared electronic file of lessons plans for the year group.

● When interactivity is encouraged, collaborative learning with lots of discussion between the children flourishes. Make sure all your children are actively participating in the lesson.

● Scanned images can be used in presentations, subject to copyright. Share images with colleagues and build up a library of suitable images for the whole school to draw upon.

● Share your experiences, for example:
  ● set up an 'Ideas' section on the school network
  ● invest in memory sticks so all ideas can be shared
  ● set aside some staff meeting time to discuss successes and disappointments, and to share information and advice.

You Can... **Use an interactive whiteboard to teach ICT**

There are many ICT applications in the classroom, and learning how to use ICT can be a daunting task. The interactive whiteboard can be used to enhance children's learning about ICT. The computer screen and its contents can be projected onto the whiteboard, enabling the whole class to benefit from the demonstration of software and hardware and their applications. Also, photos of ICT applications being used in 'real-life' situations can help to set a context for children's learning.

Thinking points

● Consider ways in which the whiteboard could be used to model ICT skills. Any application that runs on a computer can be displayed on a whiteboard, making it an ideal tool to introduce new skills in any application: spreadsheets, word processors, graphics packages, databases, modelling simulations and so on. Use the whiteboard to demonstrate specific skills and to explain independent work.

● Think about setting these ICT skills in context. For example, children may become proficient in the use of spreadsheets without understanding how spreadsheets are used in real life. Pictures of local businesses – banks, estate agents and shops – using ICT applications can be used to introduce the context of a lesson.

● The language of computers is often a barrier to progress. When performing procedural tasks, such as booting up the computer, clicking an icon or moving the cursor, talk the children through the process so they become familiar with technical terms.

Tips, ideas and activities

● As children develop confidence with computers and the complexity of their tasks increases, it becomes ever more important that they manage files and navigate the machine effectively. Use the whiteboard to model opening and saving files (with sensible names), and starting and closing programs. The teacher is a role model for children and should aim to develop pupils' proficiency with the machine as well as individual programs.

● It's frustrating when children panic because they've pressed the wrong button or seemingly lost work. Show children common mistakes and how to correct them, for example, using the back button to undo the last action.

● Demonstrate the best position to type, using both hands. Explain the layout and purpose of letter, number and function keys. Encourage children to memorise the arrangement of keys to increase their typing speed by playing Blind Man's Buff.

● When teaching upper juniors about computer control devices, show examples from real life. Take digital photos of control in action in the locality – for example, traffic lights, light sensors in street lamps and automatic doors in shops – and display them on the whiteboard to demonstrate their effect on daily life.

You Can... **Use an interactive whiteboard**

to teach shape

The whiteboard provides a wonderful opportunity to illustrate standard shapes in a colourful and interesting way. This is invaluable for lessons about shapes, but shapes are useful to illustrate other mathematical concepts, too. Shapes can easily be created and then displayed and presented ready for whole-class interaction. Creating a template with a range of standard shapes not only offers a tool for excellent and accurate presentations, but also enables the shapes to be saved for later use.

Thinking points

● Explore the different shapes that are available to you. All the common shapes are available either from the whiteboard's own software or through the use of the shape templates in Microsoft Word (see below).

● Consider different ways in which you can use shapes to illustrate other mathematical concepts. For example, shapes can be used for:

　● lessons on line symmetry, rotational symmetry and area

　● illustrating fractions in a variety of ways

　● illustrating bar charts or pictograms

　● demonstrating pattern and ratio by preparing a string of beads using circles of different colours.

Tips, ideas and activities

● To draw the common shapes using Word:

1) Click on View at the top of the screen and then click Toolbars. Tick the Drawing box. The Drawing Toolbar will appear at the bottom of the screen.

2) Click AutoShapes and point to the Basic Shapes category. Click on the shape you want.

● To insert a shape with a predefined size, click the document in which you want to display it.

● To insert a different-sized shape, drag the shape (using the surrounding handles) to the size you want. To keep the same ratio of shape, hold down Shift while you drag.

● To add colour, change borders, rotate the shape or add three-dimensional effects to it, select the object and then use the buttons on the Drawing Toolbar.

● A range of coloured shapes can be created on one page by repeating this process.

● Join two shapes together to produce more complex or more interesting shapes. For example, to create a basic house shape, drag and join a rectangle and a trapezium together. Draw the outline of each shape in the same colour and using the same colour-fill for each so that no black lines will show.

You Can... **Use an interactive whiteboard to teach line symmetry**

The whiteboard offers many opportunities to illustrate the concept of symmetry, since different images can easily be annotated. Using the whiteboard gives the whole class the opportunity to be involved in predicting and demonstrating where the reflected image will lie and drawing in lines of symmetry. Flipcharts may be printed to provide stimulating classroom displays or activities for children to complete in the main part of the lesson.

Thinking points

● As you use the whiteboard discuss the language of symmetry: for example, line of symmetry, mirror image, reflection, and mirror line.

● Think about the size of the shapes and images you are using. When using the whiteboard to show reflections, drawing in the images can be more difficult to see close to the board.

● Consider how the shapes and images are presented. For example, colour them using the Fill tool for added effect.

● Think about possible links with other subjects. For example, combine mathematics with art and encourage children to illustrate the concept of symmetry through printing, painting or paper folding and cutting.

Tips, ideas and activities

● Establish the definition and understanding of the term *symmetry* using tried-and-tested examples, such as the capital letters E and H or ladybirds and butterflies.

● Display a range of the common two-dimensional shapes, including some with no line of symmetry. Ask the children to draw in the lines of symmetry, then sort the shapes by clicking and dragging them into sets. Ask the children if the shapes in each set have anything in common. Label the sets *1 line of symmetry*, *2 lines of symmetry* and so on.

● Consolidate children's understanding of symmetry. Show a 4 × 4 squared grid in which a number of small squares have

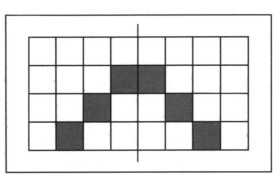

been shaded. Mark a line of symmetry and ask the children to predict where the reflected image will fall. Ask one child to draw in a second four by four square, showing the reflection with the correct squares shaded. Extend the children's understanding by moving the shape further away from the line of symmetry. Ask the children to predict the position of the reflected shape and draw it on the board. Try this again with the shape at different distances from the line of symmetry. How do the children predict where the reflected image will fall?

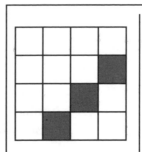
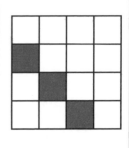

You Can... Use an interactive whiteboard for oral/mental starters

The whiteboard offers opportunities for children to become actively involved in consolidating previous learning. Activities saved from previous lessons can be modified, by changing the image or numbers involved, and used again as a starter. Starters can also be quickly prepared from scratch, and enlarged and displayed on the whiteboard. As well as using prepared and adapted files, starters can also be accessed from secondary sources, for example by using website games (copyright permitting), or interactive activities such as those found in the National Numeracy Strategy's (NNS's) Interactive Teaching Programs (www.standards.dfes.gov. uk/primary/publications/mathematics/itps/).

Thinking points

● Ensure all the children can see the whiteboard clearly, especially if software from the Internet is being used.

● Consider the timing of a starter: it is a time to consolidate previously taught objectives. If misconceptions arise, deal with them but remain aware of the time. Aim to limit the starter to a maximum of ten minutes.

● Remember: the mental starter does not have to be on the same unit of work as the main teaching activity but it should present an interesting and distinct challenge to start children thinking mathematically.

● Think about when is the best time to use an oral or mental starter. It could be used during the week that the children are taught the objectives for the first time; for test preparation; or during the week before a topic is to be introduced again at a higher level.

Tips, ideas and activities

● Enter numbers on a 4 × 5 grid, or use the number cards available from the Interactive Teaching Programs (see above). Ask questions such as:
  - *Which number is a multiple of three? How do you know? Is there only one multiple here?*
  - *Which is the largest and smallest number and which numbers lie between? How do you know this?*
  - *Order the numbers from largest to smallest. What numbers are missing?*
  - *Which number has three tens?*

● You can also ask children:
  - to read aloud different numbers
  - to add 9 to, or subtract 10 from, all the numbers
  - what facts they can you tell you about a number.

● Ask children to answer individually or as teams, and with or without 'Show me' resources, such as individual whiteboards or number cards.

● Use the Stopwatch or Egg Timer tools (usually available through the whiteboard's own software) to time answers. When a number is discussed, highlight or erase it from the grid.

● Create similar starter activities using, for example, a range of two-dimensional and three-dimensional shapes, analogue and digital clocks for calculating time or a display of British coins to reinforce calculations involving money.

● Save starters as flipcharts, to be used again as starters or plenary activities.

You Can... **Use an interactive whiteboard to interpret charts and graphs**

An interactive whiteboard is an effective tool in teaching the data-handling cycle: starting with a question, collecting data, processing and presenting the data, interpreting it and then answering the initial question. Traditionally, much time is spent collecting data and transferring it to a visual representation in the form of a chart or graph. Consequently, less time is given to interpretation, usually the weakest part of the data-handling process. Whiteboard software enables you to collate data into a table and quickly generate a bar chart or block graph, leaving more time to focus on data interpretation.

Tips, ideas and activities

● Copy, paste or scan a bar chart or graph and hide its title. Ask pairs to discuss what the graph reveals. Scribe their suggestions. Ask the children to suggest a title for the representation.

● Copy, paste or scan a bar chart or graph and hide the axes labels and scale. Ask what the graph might show. Incorrect responses may provide excellent discussion points, for example, a bar chart with only ten bars will not generally be used to illustrate monthly events.

● Display a line graph and interpret it in relation to its title. Does the graph suggest that one of the variables is increasing, decreasing or is steady in relation to the other? Ask pairs to record in no more than three sentences what the graph represents. Make a note of their suggestions. Repeat with a similar set of data and encourage children to make comparisons between the graphs.

● Display a bar chart vertically. Ask children to base their interpretations on the labelled axes and scales. Collect feedback and then display the same data in a horizontal bar chart. Ask pupils to interpret again. Children may not immediately realise that it is the same data and may be less familiar with horizontal bar charts.

● To draw charts and graphs for the whiteboard with Excel:
 1) Open Excel and input the data. The data that is independent, eg that will form the horizontal axis on a bar chart, should be put under column A. Other data should be put under column B.

Thinking points

● Think about how the whiteboard can support you in each stage of the data-handling cycle. Model the cycle with an example generated by the class, for example, children's favourite television programmes. Start with obvious interpretations, such as the most or least popular. Then move on to considering programmes in between. Consider whether the interpretations are relevant and link back to the question. If children are asked to nominate two favourite programmes, how will the graph change?

● Explore data representations from secondary sources. Subject to copyright, weather, financial or medical graphs can be found on websites or in newspapers.

● Explore different options for drawing graphs. The website http://nces.ed.gov/nceskids/graphing/ provides a tool for drawing graphs, alternatively, Excel may be used to draw graphs quickly.

● Use previous National Test questions (taken from QCA's Test Base CD) to illustrate data interpretation. These can be displayed and annotated so that the whole class can view the graphs easily.

2) Highlight all of the data by holding down the mouse and dragging it across the data.

3) Click Insert (top line on menu), then Chart. On the screen a box with a list of charts plus small illustrations of what they look like will appear.

4) Decide which type of chart you would like (bar chart, pie chart and so on) and select.

5) If you choose Bar chart, then a range of different styles of bar chart will appear. Choose the one you would like by clicking on it. Click Next and the bar chart will appear. Click Next again then click Finish.

6) The bar chart has small squares surrounding it. In this mode you can change titles or labels on axes.

7) To remove the box saying *Series 1* click inside it, then press Delete.

8) To give the graph a title click in the very top row (next to fx) and type in your title.

9) Click anywhere outside the bar chart area and the title will appear. Click your mouse on the title until you see the cross sign. Click again and the title can be dragged to where you need it.

10) Click inside the white border. You can then copy and paste your chart into a Word document on the whiteboard.

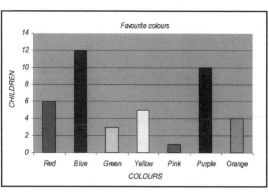

To produce a pie chart or line graph select either at point 4 in the process and repeat the procedures.

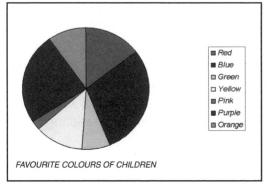

FAVOURITE COLOURS OF CHILDREN

If you want to print straight from Excel rather than copy to word then select *Set print area* before printing.

Note: This chart drawing facility will do what you ask it to do, even if this is not mathematically sound.

You Can... **Use an interactive whiteboard to demonstrate spreadsheets**

Getting to grips with new software and applications is a perfect way to use interactive whiteboards. It enables whole class teaching, modelling and interaction to take place in a supported environment prior to independent activity. Spreadsheets are a good example of this. The whiteboard will enable you to model the whole process of using a spreadsheet, using the language of spreadsheets as you do so. Spreadsheets have a wide range of applications in mathematics and other subjects and are used in 'real life' contexts both in and out of school.

Thinking points

● Teach spreadsheets through another subject, such as geography. Use contexts that children will find interesting and challenging so that there is real purpose to learning.

● Show children how spreadsheets are used in 'real life'. Ask people who use spreadsheets to speak to the children (for example, the school secretary).

● Special events in the school year may provide purposeful links to spreadsheets, for example, class trips, refurbishing a classroom or a Christmas party. Model how a spreadsheet can be used to calculate costs, or keep check on payments.

● Make sure that your whiteboard is properly oriented to display the spreadsheets. Highlighting cells and other processes can be tricky when boards are not calibrated accurately.

● Prepare a range of spreadsheets to familiarise children with spreadsheet conventions – this is particularly useful for less confident learners.

● When children use spreadsheets confidently, set challenges to use them for open-ended problem-solving activities as well as straightforward calculations.

Tips, ideas and activities

● Display a blank spreadsheet. Explain its structure. Ask children what the Task Bar shows. Explore Toolbars, predicting the use of each icon. Ensure children know how to read cell references and practise locating and highlighting cells. Encourage children to use correct terminology.

● Model the use of spreadsheets: opening programs, opening and saving files and entering data and formulae. Discuss spreadsheet titles and column labels.

● Enter data using the floating keyboard. Explain the difference between numeric data and text and how spreadsheets use and represent them.

● Model setting up spreadsheets:
  ○ to calculate the perimeter of various shapes. Discuss appropriate titles and the number of columns needed. Show children how to enter an addition formula to find totals.
  ○ to calculate the area of simple shapes, using a multiplication formula. Ask children to measure objects and enter data. Challenge more able children to calculate areas of compound shapes, which will involve two-step operations to find the total.

● Teach older children more involved applications, using the context of measures. Model setting up a spreadsheet to convert units of measurement, for example miles to kilometres. Model how to produce graphs, to develop data-handling skills.

You Can... **Use an interactive whiteboard for 100 square activities**

The main advantage of using a 100 square on an interactive whiteboard is flexibility. You are not constrained to the 10×10 pattern and can create any number of squares (or rectangles) to fit the needs of your lesson. Sequences of numbers and times-table patterns using hundreds, thousands, negative numbers and decimals can be displayed. Numbers can also be removed to create a partially completed square. Finally, the 100 square takes up no space in the class and always presents a clean, sharp image that can be coloured to fit the needs of your class.

Thinking points

● Ask yourself whether your projector is bright enough for the children to see the number square clearly. Some projectors make it hard for children to see the numbers. Also, some programs default to a square that is quite small relative to other interactive whiteboard resources.

● If you have dyslexic or colour-blind children (more common in boys) in your class you may want to colour the background blue with white digits, as this colour combination is easier for them to read.

Tips, ideas and activities

● Fill the squares that surround a target number in black. The Fill button usually includes a Paint Brush tool, which can be used to automatically format all the lines or areas selected.

● If your class computer or whiteboard software does not have a number square tool, download the Number grid program from the National Numeracy Strategy's Interactive Teaching Programs (www.standards.dfes.gov.uk/primary/publications/ mathematics/itps). It has five main functions:
  ● Mask – this allows the user to hide certain numbers.
  ● Primes – pressing this highlights the primes in your grid.
  ● Start number – the number that your grid will start at.
  ● Columns – this will change the number of columns on your grid.
  ● Multiples – this allows you to focus on different multiples.

● A Number Grid manual is also available on the ITP website, see above for web address. This provides an overview of the key features of the program.

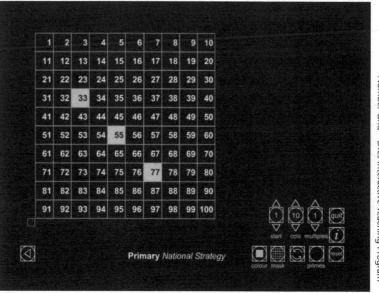

Number Grid – Dfes Interactive Teaching Program

You Can... Use an interactive whiteboard for number line activities

Children who demonstrate a clear understanding of the size of a number relative to its position in the number system have grasped the concept of place value. They should then be able to count forward and back in different steps and order and position numbers confidently. The use of the whiteboard allows these processes to be taught and assessed in an interactive way. There is a range of on-screen number lines and place value cards, found on whiteboard menus and from the NNS Interactive Teaching Programs (www.standards.dfes.gov.uk/primary/publications/ mathematics/itps/).

Thinking points

- Interactive number lines can be used to support children in understanding the process of ordering numbers, and understanding the size of a number in relation to other numbers. Consider what children may already know and need to understand:

  - Can children read, write and say two- and three-digit numbers?

  - Can children position 71 and 17 on the same number line? Can they identify the difference between the numbers, the place value of each digit and the relative size of the numbers?

- Children need a picture of the ordered numbers in their heads. Make sure that you use a mixture of complete, demarcated and blank interactive number lines to support children's understanding of number.

- Think about different ways in which interactive number lines can be used in your lessons: for example, counting, performing mental calculations and jotting down intermediate calculations.

Tips, ideas and activities

- Position a marker on a number line and hide the number. Challenge children to estimate and then accurately work out what the number is, before revealing it.

- Produce a blank number line and generate ten two- and three-digit numbers. Children then position the smallest and largest numbers at either end of the line and order the remaining numbers. Alternatively, display a demarcated blank line and use the Zoom facility to highlight the required section required.

- For a quick mental starter, display an unordered number line and ask children to drag individual number cards to the correct position and complete any missing numbers.

- Use a blank number line to demonstrate addition; subtraction by counting on or back to the nearest tens number; and early division by 'chunking' back in multiples. Use the Snapshot tool to capture annotations for use in future sessions.

- Use a blank or demarcated number line to position a series of fractions dragged from the menu. Demonstrate converting fractions to decimals with the use of the on-screen calculator, and position these along the line.

- Prepare a completed number line demarcated in tens, for example 900 to 1100. Count on and back in tens, bridging 100s and 1000s.

You Can... **Use an interactive whiteboard to illustrate fractions**

The key to understanding and later calculating with fractions is to identify the whole – whether the whole is an object, shape, quantity or number – and then to identify how many parts of that whole make up the fraction. Dividing, moving or grouping images or shapes can be effectively demonstrated using the interactive whiteboard.

Thinking points

● Use the whiteboard to:

● illustrate the concept of a fraction: that it is a part of something whole and that the parts must be equal

● link fractions to division

● show the relative size of a fraction in relation to other fractions and whole numbers

● practise the terms numerator and denominator

● show that it is easier first to find one part of a fraction.

● Check that your whiteboard includes a Fractions tool, which gives fractions in correct notation.

● Investigate the same fraction in three different ways in one lesson, the importance of identifying the whole will be reinforced. Choose a simple fraction with an easily divisible denominator (for example, $\frac{3}{4}$). In the plenary session, discuss whether it is easier to find the fraction of a shape, a number of objects or a straightforward number. Extend children's understanding by using fractions with a different denominator, for example $\frac{3}{5}$.

Tips, ideas and activities

● Demonstrate fractions of shapes:

● Select a simple two-dimensional shape from the AutoShapes tool in Word (for example, a rectangle).

● Ask pupils if one quarter can be easily shown on this shape.

● Ask whether the shape can be divided into equal parts in more than one way and if there are easier shapes with which to illustrate this fraction.

● Discuss how many quarters make one whole.

● Following the discussion, demonstrate some of the ways that $\frac{3}{4}$ can be illustrated, or ask children to show this on the whiteboard.

● Demonstrate fractions of objects:

● Select an object (from Clip Art in Word or from the whiteboard Images Bank).

● Copy and paste the object several times, making sure the number of objects is a multiple of the denominator.

● Emphasise that the collection of objects is the whole.

● Ask pairs to find $\frac{1}{4}$ of this collection using their small whiteboards for jotting.

● Then ask them to demonstrate how they grouped the objects and discuss any mental and written division methods they used. Use the Pen tool to highlight the children's responses.

● Next, ask children to demonstrate how they found $\frac{3}{4}$ of the number of objects by coming to the board and highlighting or circling their selections.

● Repeat the above process with a number, for example 24.

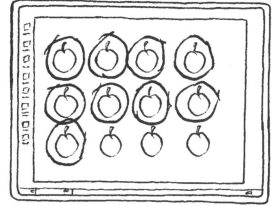

You Can... **Use an interactive whiteboard to demonstrate angles**

Measuring and calculating angles can be especially difficult for children to grasp, more so than units of measurement for capacity, length and weight, which involve tangible amounts. That is why it is important to demonstrate angles in a variety of very visual ways. The whiteboard is an ideal medium for this, providing a platform for modelling, practice and refinement of techniques. It enables you to introduce the idea of scales, using the protractor on the whiteboard, and to model measuring angles. You can also use digital photos of angles in the environment, to place problem-solving in context.

Thinking points

● Introduce children to scales on the protractor on the whiteboard. Several programs are available with large angle measures, for example, *What's My Angle?*, from the DfES's Using ICT to Support Primary Mathematics pack. If you don't have a suitable program, scan a plastic protractor and paste the image into Microsoft Word. Use the Pen tool to draw attention to scales and intervals.

● Think about how you will verbalise every step of the procedure when you use the whiteboard to model a technique or problem-solving method. Spell out what you are doing to help children develop the language of angles and reinforce the procedural steps involved.

● Reflect on the interests of the class when making resources for the whiteboard, as children become proficient in measuring and calculating angles, present problems set in context to develop children's problem-solving skills. For example, angles for measurement could represent the path of a ball kicked from the sideline.

Tips, ideas and activities

● Model how to measure and estimate angles using 'Calculating Angles', one of the free NNS Interactive Teaching Programs (www.standards.dfes.gov.uk/primary/publications/mathematics/itps/). With this program you can: measure angles up to 90°, 180°, or 360°; calculate angles within triangles and quadrilaterals; or solve problems. It also contains a transparent protractor, which can be lifted and rotated around the board.

● When children can confidently name angles of different sizes, ask them to take digital photographs of angles in the school environment. Display the photos on the whiteboard for discussion. Use the Pen or Highlighter tools to draw on the angles to illustrate them.

● Import digital photographs of angles into Microsoft Word and ask volunteers to estimate the angle and then label it as acute, obtuse or a right angle.

● Develop problem-solving skills by investigating angles within shapes. Remind the children that angles in triangles have a sum of 180°. In Microsoft Word, use the AutoShapes tool to paste triangles on to the page. Write in two angles and ask the children to calculate the third angle. Use the same idea for quadrilaterals or other polygons.

You Can... **Use an interactive whiteboard to investigate multiples**

Most children become familiar with multiples through counting. The interactive whiteboard can provide visual activities to support oral exercises – for example, counting using tools such as an interactive counting stick – so that multiples are highlighted when counting. The advantage of the whiteboard is that visual 'proofs' can be produced quickly, for example by colouring numbers within a 100 square when a multiple occurs. In addition, numbers can easily be enlarged, reduced, annotated or hidden.

Thinking points

● Establish the definition and understanding of the term 'multiple' and 'factor' using examples of known times tables facts, for example, the two- or five-times tables.

● When the children count numbers aloud, display a large coloured grid and point to each number as it is spoken – this will be particularly useful for children with English as an additional language and children with special needs. Exposure to the grid over time will support visual learners, helping them to memorise patterns that will become triggers to recall multiples.

● Revise the rules of divisibility to support identifying factors of three-digit numbers.

● Present the multiple alongside its two factors, or as a triangle of facts. This will help children who may be able to recite multiples but struggle to relate this back to a multiplication or division fact.

Tips, ideas and activities

● Draw a counting stick made from ten coloured sections. Count on and back, writing the multiples on the sections. Play a memory game by showing numbers and then hiding them. Alternatively, order a set of multiples along a line.

● Show ten numbers and ask children to identify those in a particular times table. Erase numbers from the screen as the children respond.

● Colour a 100 square or 200 grid as children count on and back in specific multiples. Use different colours for each times table. Investigate the numbers with the most colours and those remaining uncoloured (the prime numbers).

● Generate ten two- and three-digit numbers. Investigate whether these are multiples of four and five. Check the factors of larger numbers using the on-screen calculator. Display a Venn diagram with one circle representing multiples of four and the other multiples of five. Insert the ten numbers in the correct section of the Venn diagram. Extend the activity by discussing where to position a number that is not a multiple of either four or five. Using different pairs of multiples display the multiples in a table, grid or as a Carroll diagram.

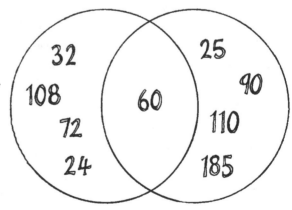

● Use the constant function key of on-screen calculator to count up and back in multiples.

You Can... **Use an interactive whiteboard to create collaborative poems**

Shared and guided writing on the whiteboard enhances children's writing experiences. The whiteboard helps to stimulate discussion about poems, looking at different aspects such as rhyming structure, imagery or word choices. It enables children to watch you model reading and writing poetry, and to collaborate in creating a poem in a supportive environment. Shared work can be edited, saved and printed. Children love seeing their work displayed on the whiteboard, enabling you to celebrate success while presenting good poems as a model for others to follow.

Thinking points

● Subject to copyright restrictions, look for suitable poems to present to the class. Scan or type them into PowerPoint or Word to present on the whiteboard. Discuss different poems and challenge the quality of children's responses. Give them vocabulary to enhance their comments.

● Think about how to model the writing process, either starting with a blank page or supporting the less able with a supportive scaffold. Create writing frames using PowerPoint or Microsoft Word, saving them for later use.

● Explain choices about vocabulary, rhyming structure or imagery when you create a poem on the whiteboard. Use a regular repeating pattern when modelling poetry writing. This will help children follow your lead and guide their own structured writing efforts.

● Use the floating keyboard to type when modelling writing strategies on the whiteboard. Alternatively, write or draw freehand using the Pen tool (handwriting recognition software can be used to convert this into typewritten text).

Tips, ideas and activities

● Use the Highlighter or Pen tools to draw attention to notable parts of poems.

● Prepare a PowerPoint presentation of a poem, illustrated with Clip Art.

● Remove descriptive words or phrases in a poem and complete it as a whole-class activity. Encourage the children to think of the imagery they want to create in the reader's mind. Alternatively, work with them during shared reading (or guided tasks) to complete the poem.

● Write the first verse of a poem together in shared writing and ask the children to continue it as independent work.

● Write a collaborative alphabet zoo poem, using alliterative phrases. Prepare a page of animals in PowerPoint or Notebook using Clip Art (available through Word or from the whiteboard Images Bank). Assign each pair of children a different letter (more able children could be given a letter each). Start the ball rolling by writing *Amazing anteaters ambling* on the whiteboard. Encourage the children to write a phrase for their letter, for example, *busy bees buzzing, cautious cats climbing* and so on. Collect the phrases and write them on the board. Ask the children to comment on why they think their poem is successful.

You Can... **Use an interactive whiteboard to interact with texts**

One of the obvious advantages of using an interactive whiteboard is the facility to display text on screen of any size, colour and font. It is possible to enlarge and illustrate text in a way that a photocopier or big book would never be able to do, and to present it as a sharp, clear image. Adults and children can interact with the text by highlighting, editing, copying and pasting any section. A huge advantage over using conventional texts is that when a mistake is made the user can undo the previous command to remove it.

Thinking points

● Consider how much text you need to display. If the whole class has to read a lengthy extract, this may be done better through individual readers. Use the whiteboard for smaller extracts that link directly to the teaching objective.

● When using a website, consider the content of the text: Is the language appropriate for the children in your class and is it aimed at a primary audience? Can the children see the website clearly? Does the text meet the needs of the teaching objective? Do you need all of the text or just part of it?

● Consider the copyright implications before copying, pasting and manipulating any published texts. Check the front of a book or a website homepage for any restrictions before using a text in this way.

Tips, ideas and activities

● Create cloze procedure activities on the whiteboard. Copy or type a text on to the board and edit out key words, such as adjectives, asking the class to suggest a range of alternatives. Alternatively, the key words could be covered and then revealed, using the annotation tools.

● Enlarge text on a website by clicking on View at the top of the web browser and selecting Text Size. All web browsers automatically default to a medium view and there are usually two larger sizes available.

● Edit children's work on the whiteboard with the whole class. This can be a very useful activity, particularly if there has been a clear set of 'editing objectives' given to the class at the start of the lesson.

● Interactive texts often contain hyperlinks (coloured and underlined text that takes the user to a different document or web page). Be careful with your use of hyperlinked texts in class as they can often be unnecessarily diverting.

You Can... **Use an interactive whiteboard for whole-class reading**

Choices of text for shared and guided reading are often limited to published big books. With an interactive whiteboard, choices become almost limitless, especially for schools with Internet access. Texts displayed electronically can be manipulated, edited or annotated, subject to any copyright restrictions. Unlike books, it is possible to save changes whilst keeping a copy of the original version. Versions can also be printed off for investigation, or used as a writing prompt.

Thinking points

● Subject to copyright, passages of texts from books can be copied and imported into programs like Microsoft Word or PowerPoint. Pictures can be scanned and placed to match the original design.

● Carefully chosen Internet pages make excellent shared texts (again, copyright permitting). There are many exciting and relevant sites that offer a wide variety of text types (for example, the BBC web site, www.bbc.co.uk). Use this content 'live', or, if the website is not subject to copyright restrictions, copy it by clicking Print Screen and pasting into Word.

● Suitable newspaper material can be hard to find. The website www.thenewspaper.org.uk is written specifically for children, including child-friendly articles that use all the features of traditional papers. Find relevant articles using the search, and then capture and display them on the whiteboard.

● Take time to ensure the whiteboard is correctly configured, so that any annotations or marks made using the pens will be precise.

● Think about the size of the extract or web page and adjust View as required.

Tips, ideas and activities

● Control the amount of text visible with the Screen Reveal or Curtain tool. This has a grab handle at the top and by dragging down using the whiteboard pen it reveals text line-by-line or paragraph-by-paragraph. This is an invaluable tool for focusing attention on each part of the text and enables slow readers to keep up.

● Imported texts can be highlighted during a shared investigation. Click on the Highlight tool and drag it across the key words you wish to focus upon. This tool can be used in many ways: identifying use of different punctuation; locating word classes; identifying figurative language; finding links between paragraphs; uncovering sentence structures; highlighting spelling patterns, plurals or use of apostrophes. Having seen this process modelled, pages can be printed for children to investigate and highlight by hand independently.

● Use the Pen tool in different colours to note features of the text, for example connectives, as it is read. Annotation on the whiteboard is easy. Use pens to circle, underline, or draw arrows to anything on the page – words, paragraphs, headings, illustrations or captions. Also, encourage the children to come to the board and use the tools. Annotations can be saved, printed or removed as necessary.

You Can... **Use an interactive whiteboard to stimulate creative writing**

For most children, learning to write creatively is an exciting process. It involves thinking imaginatively, as well as using other literacy skills to structure written work. Some children find it difficult to generate ideas and need a strong stimulus to inspire them to write creatively. A stimulus could be a sound, a picture or a moving image (video clip). The whiteboard is capable of manipulating all of these elements and is therefore a very useful tool for stimulating, as well as helping to structure, children's writing.

Thinking points

● Consider the use of drama to scaffold children's written work. Drama encourages children to step into the unknown. Mystical and mundane objects can be created, and entire worlds can evolve, through the power of the imagination.

● Consider which is the most important element – spelling, punctuation and grammar or the development of their initial ideas – when asking children to write creatively.

● Consider how you might use the whiteboard to build a whole-class story, for example, writing or annotating suggestions for developing the story, presenting alternative endings, adding Clip Art illustrations or adding sounds for dramatic effect.

● Reflect on the powerful effect the spoken word has on children's written work. Encourage the children to verbalise their ideas before writing them down. The challenge is then to transform the verbal into a written form that uses an interesting range of vocabulary and captivates the reader.

Tips, ideas and activities

● Many stories, in particular fairy stories, enable children to delve deep into the world of make-believe. Pictures and illustrations often help children to describe this world and the places within it. Draw a land map of a fairy story on a blank flipchart and mark the places where characters live. Draw in paths or roads for the characters to venture down. Ask questions to help the children create scenes from the story.

● Children often recognise good ideas that they could use themselves when they read another child's work. It can also provide a starting point for less able children. Scan a child's piece of writing into a blank flipchart and read it through with the whole class. Challenge the children to find a sentence they really like, or that is important to the story, and to explain why. Challenge them to improve the work by asking, *How can we make it even better?* Follow their suggestions, making annotations with the Pen or Highlighter tool.

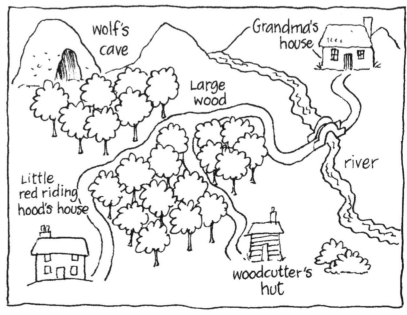

You Can... Use an interactive whiteboard to discuss types of speech

Despite living in an age of emails and text messages, the spoken word remains the most popular form of communication: stories are told, messages given, information conveyed and learning shared through speech. Children should be encouraged to introduce dialogue into their creative writing. This will help them to build interest and tension and to develop interaction between characters. The whiteboard is a great tool for sharing and interrogating all types of spoken communication.

Thinking points

● Consider the different forms that speech can take. Explore the use of indirect speech or reported speech. Explain to the children that reported speech details what was said without using the exact words. Consider the use of caption cartoons to help the children think of what may have been said.

● Children generate a lot of 'talk' in role-play activities. Think about how you might use the whiteboard to capture this direct speech in different ways.

● Consider using different ways of representing direct speech. Speech bubbles can be used to show the actual words spoken, whereas thought bubbles give the reader an insight into unspoken thoughts.

Tips, ideas and activities

● Digital images are a great way to excite and develop dialogue in children's writing. Collect photographs of famous people in different poses. Ask members of staff to pose for photographs, perhaps exaggerating their facial expressions and gestures. Insert the photographs into a blank flipchart. Ask the children to think of what the person could be saying. It could be as humorous or realistic as you wish!

● Choose a topic of interest and invite a volunteer to stand up and say something on the subject. Write this in a speech bubble on the whiteboard. As a class, discuss how this comment could be edited or rewritten. The whiteboard offers the opportunity for instant feedback and the development of an idea without the need for lots of resource preparation. It is also open to a range of easy adaptation by saving and modifying the children's work.

● Encourage the children to write direct speech in different ways. Insert two pictures of mobile phones. Draw a box around the two phones. Ask the children to think of a scenario where two people are sending text messages to each other. Ask the children to work in pairs to write the text messages that would appear on the mobiles.

● Align a word processor and a media player side-by-side on the computer desktop. Play a scene from a video or DVD. Use the pause button to give you time to transcribe the dialogue from the scene (this could be prepared in advance). Then ask the children to add the speech marks and punctuation in the correct places. Ask individual children to predict what happens next.

You Can... **Use an interactive whiteboard to sequence stories**

Sequencing skills are vital in helping children to understand story structure. Instead of making and laminating sequencing cards and asking children to stick the cards in order with Blu-Tack, the same task can be created and developed using the interactive whiteboard. This activity shows you how to make an interactive activity in which the children come to the whiteboard and sequence parts of a story.

Thinking points

● The best applications to use for this activity are Microsoft PowerPoint, Publisher or the whiteboard software. Microsoft Word does not allow you to manipulate text as easily.

● The above applications allow you to add colours, backgrounds, sounds and Clip Art to your files. It is worth considering this. Although it will involve extra preparation time, once the files are created they can be saved and re-used, thus saving time in the long run.

● A similar activity can be prepared for sequencing words in a sentence.

● Back up files regularly on to a CD-ROM, memory stick or floppy disc. There is nothing more frustrating than losing all of your hard work by forgetting this basic routine.

Tips, ideas and activities

● To prepare the activity:
  ● Insert a text box and type in the first sentence from the story. Highlight the text and click Format and then Font. Select an appropriate font style and size. Choose a type size of at least 32 point and a child-friendly font such as Sassoon Primary or Comic Sans. Put a border round the text by double clicking the text box, or right-clicking the mouse and going to Format Text Box in the drop-down menu. Change the option No Line to a colour. Repeat the process on the same slide for each sentence in the story. Use a different border colour for each text box. Drag and drop each text box into position.

● To use the activity in class:
  ● Open the pre-prepared PowerPoint slide. Do not run it as a slide show because the children will not be able to move the text boxes. Close the columns on the left- and right-hand sides by clicking on the little crosses in the corners. This will make the slide bigger. Ask the children to read the sentences. Ask a child to come to the board and use the Pen tool to move the first text box into position. Repeat until all slides are in position.

> They liked to eat porridge for breakfast.
>
> Once upon a time there were three bears who lived in the woods.
>
> While they were out, a little girl with golden hair came walking by.
>
> Their porridge was too hot so they decided to go for a walk in the woods while it cooled down.

You Can... Use an interactive whiteboard to write super sentences

The interactive whiteboard offers tremendous benefits in terms of text editing, proofreading, formulating sentences and stimulating creative writing. Parts of speech, accurate punctuation, spelling and letter formation can all be taught very effectively and in an interactive way. The whiteboard affords a range of strategies for showing best practice, modelled work and experimentation, supporting the writing process at every stage. The sheer range of possibilities, even when working with just a simple sentence, makes the interactive whiteboard an invaluable addition to any literacy lesson.

Thinking points

● Before producing a piece of text for a whole-class session, think about how it will help the children learn as well as how it will supply what you need to teach.

● If you are preparing sentences before a lesson, it is possible to type them using Microsoft Word and then reformat them into the whiteboard's own software (for example, '.xbk' for SMART Notebook, or '.flp' for Promethean ACTIVprimary). In this way, text can be more easily manipulated on the whiteboard.

● It is not always necessary to create sentences from scratch – consider selecting sentences or paragraphs taken from current work or linked to cross-curricular topics.

● Plan all of the potential uses that you could make with a piece of text and prioritise your ideas. Remember that the whole-class session should only form a small part of a well-structured and well-paced lesson.

● Make a habit of collecting pictures that will promote discussion and stimulate simple sentences.

Tips, ideas and activities

● Use the Pen or Highlighter tools to draw over and hide words in a comprehension (cloze) exercise. Use the Eraser tool to reveal the words or phrases as they are identified.

● Type or write some sentences on the whiteboard that include the word *nice*, for example, *The nice policeman gave directions* or *The view of the bay was very nice*. Highlight the word *nice* and ask the children for alternatives. Annotate their suggestions on the board. This type of activity could also be used to introduce new vocabulary to replace less interesting or descriptive alternatives.

● Type a sentence and make deliberate mistakes for the children to identify.

● Type a number of sentences in the format *Paul kicks a football*. Challenge individual children to come to the board to annotate the verbs, changing them from present tense to past or future tense. Encourage the children to write their own sentences in this format. Include some simple Clip Art to stimulate interest.

● Demonstrate writing sentences on the whiteboard using the Pen tool. This tool's facility to change line width, colour and style enables clear demonstration of letter formation and makes it ideal for spelling activities linked to learning to join letters correctly.

You Can... **Use an interactive whiteboard to teach punctuation**

Many children struggle with accurate punctuation and it can be frustrating and time-consuming to correct repeated mistakes. The whiteboard affords a range of very effective strategies for showing best practice, for modelling work and for experimenting with punctuation use. Extracts from books and other sources can be scanned into Microsoft PowerPoint or Word and projected on to the whiteboard, creating a very visible shared text. Using the whiteboard's interactive potential, you can support the writing process at every stage.

Thinking points

- Consider at the planning stage how you will use the whiteboard to teach punctuation. Organise files for saving prepared lessons and remember to save them under easily recognisable names.

- Punctuation can be inserted using the Pen tool, which makes the whiteboard excellent for shared writing. The floating keyboard may also be used, although asking the children to type might slow the lesson down. It is therefore best to limit the use of the keyboard to work on short texts or extracts.

- The whiteboard provides an easy way to improve children's writing in front of the whole class, so that everyone can benefit from the comments. However, be sensitive if using children's own work to correct errors, and choose children who are confident enough to receive constructive criticism. Also, always remember to praise and celebrate success at the same time as correcting or improving upon children's work.

Tips, ideas and activities

- During shared reading, look at a text in which the author expertly uses the range of punctuation your lesson will focus on. Identify and draw attention to punctuation using the Highlighter or Pen tools.

- Remove all the punctuation from a text (or a selected type of punctuation). Read the text, emphasising difficulties with meaning and the lack of pauses. Re-read it, asking children to show where, and what type of, punctuation should be inserted. Ask them to justify their choices, explaining what function the punctuation will serve.

- Model the use of punctuation during shared and guided work. Use the whiteboard pens (or the floating keyboard) to write a passage and talk about what you are doing. Demonstrate that writing is a thought-out process, in which vocabulary, sentence structure and punctuation choices are linked to purpose.

- Use good examples of punctuation in children's work in the plenary session. Read the piece with the whole class and ask children to comment on how the punctuation was used and its effect.

- Model how to edit completed pieces of writing. Use coloured pens to annotate and mark in changes. Make explicit choices about vocabulary, sentence structures, paragraphing and punctuation usage. As children become more experienced, allow them to suggest improvements that can be made.

You Can... **Use an interactive whiteboard to demonstrate word processing**

In its earliest form, the word processor enabled children to translate their work from the written into the printed word. As a result, even the slowest writers were able to produce and present work of a high quality. Since its introduction, the word processor has evolved and is now capable of integrating pictures, drawing up tables, and much more. Using a whiteboard will help you to demonstrate to children the full potential of this simple but powerful application.

Thinking points

● Consider demonstrating the use of the thesaurus and spell check facilities, to assist children with their editing skills. This is a good opportunity to model good practice and provides a focus for whole-class discussion on the use of vocabulary in general, and synonyms in particular.

● Think about the cross-curricular links that can be made when using a word processor. Many literacy, ICT and foundation objectives can be met at the same time, through the same activity.

● Consider using the Highlighter tool to identify adjectives, powerful verbs, subordinate clauses – the possibilities are endless! Select a different colour for each.

● Encourage the children to think about the effect words can have on a piece of writing. Encourage them to think about why they might use effects such as emboldening or underlining text.

Tips, ideas and activities

● Type in a passage of text that includes spelling and grammar mistakes. Ask the children to explain how the computer shows them that a spelling mistake has been made. Discuss the differences between red and green underlining in a Word document. Show them how to use Find and Replace, to look for common errors.

● Type in an appropriate passage of text and show the children how to use the thesaurus to find alternative words. Demonstrate how careful word choices can enhance written work.

● Demonstrate how to use different text editing features of the word processor. For example, display a passage of text that includes a dialogue between two people and type it in. Ask the children to identify the words spoken by each character. Once they have done this, highlight and copy the lines of speech, pasting them in the format of a play script. Show the children how to use appropriate text editing features, such as italics for emphasis, or bold to highlight the character names.

● Model the use of various features of the word processor, such as inserting Clip Art, or drawing tables. Verbalise what you are doing as you do it. Discuss with children when such features might be useful, and what their effect is.

You Can... **Use an interactive whiteboard to make an electronic book**

Children love to see their work on display. What better motivation could you provide than displaying their work in an electronic book that can be viewed on the interactive whiteboard? Electronic books can be produced easily, using either the software provided with your whiteboard, or Microsoft PowerPoint. You can use electronic books as a record of the children's work in a particular topic and also for assessment purposes. They also look very impressive as a rolling display at parents' evenings!

Thinking points

● Decide whether the book is to contain photographs or illustrations. If the scanner is located on another machine, consider how you are going to transfer scanned images to the whiteboard computer. Good quality scanned images can be much larger than the capacity of a floppy disk. Connecting the scanner to the computer that controls the whiteboard may be the easiest option.

● Digital photographs of children's work should be taken with a reasonably high resolution, to ensure the image is of a good quality when it is displayed.

● When evaluating children's work that has been produced electronically, point out how easy it is to edit the work compared with editing a paper-based version.

● If any of the children's work is going to be displayed outside school for any reason, for example on the school website, make sure that parental consent is given.

Tips, ideas and activities

● Scan a collection of the children's artwork, based on a particular theme. Insert each image on to a new page of the interactive whiteboard software, resizing as necessary. Let the children think of a name for their pieces of artwork and type it underneath using the keyboard.

● Microsoft PowerPoint can be used to create an electronic book in the shared writing session. Insert a number of pages, using a template that provides space for an image and a text block. Use Clip Art, photographs or children's drawings and ask the children to think of and then type in appropriate text. Read and evaluate the end product as a whole class, and edit it accordingly.

● Ask the children to work in groups to pick out their best pieces of work for a particular topic. Photograph or scan the work chosen by the group. Insert the images into the interactive whiteboard software and resize them so that they can be rearranged. The children can further enhance their work by adding more explanatory text.

You Can... **Use an interactive whiteboard to explain scientific concepts**

Using pictures and text on an interactive whiteboard is an ideal way to help children learn scientific words. The whiteboard provides an easily accessible visual aid that can be used throughout a science lesson. Microsoft Word's Clip Gallery offers a wide range of images which can then be labelled. Images can be drawn from other sources, subject to copyright restrictions, such as books and websites, that will also be suitable for the vocabulary you want to introduce. Video clips that explain scientific processes provide a further opportunity for consolidation of key concepts, and are particularly useful for more visual learners.

Thinking points

● Ensure images match the related word and are used appropriately. For example, a picture of a snake as an example of a 'predator' is potentially confusing, as snakes can also be 'prey' to hawks and other birds. Clip Art images can be pasted on the whiteboard and labelled using the arrows from the Drawing Toolbar and text boxes. For example, label *leaves, flower, stem,* and *roots* for a plant, or label different body parts on a human body.

● Think how to make the task interactive. For example, rather than pre-labelling your Clip Art image, children could be asked to drag and position the labels during the lesson.

● Frame questions carefully to ensure children can answer using the correct vocabulary on the screen. To assess individual children's understanding, ask them to write their answers on individual whiteboards.

Tips, ideas and activities

● Ask children to use new words in a sentence, or highlight them in a text extract and explain their meanings.

● Use a video clip, for example a seed germinating and growing into a plant, to explain a scientific process. Pause the video so that correct words can be reviewed and questions asked, for example: *What is that part of the plant called? What is going to happen next?*

● Prepare a cloze procedure text using whiteboard software. Cover up the key scientific words that are being taught. (Microsoft Word Shape tools can also be used for this purpose.) Read the sentence and ask children to choose the correct scientific word. Reveal the word to check if they are correct.

● Make a concept cartoon using pictures from Clip Art and the speech bubble tool from the Drawing Toolbar or Resource Library. For example, show a child standing by a tank of water and a piece of wood. Add a speech bubble: *I think it will sink because it is too large.* Reinforce the words *floating* and *sinking* using the concept cartoon. Ask children if the child is correct.

● Make text boxes containing key words on one side of the page, and text boxes containing their explanation on the other side of the page. Ask children to link them using the arrow drawing tool from the Drawing Toolbar.

● Demonstrate making a concept or mind map. List the key words. Use the arrow from the drawing tool bar to link ideas. Insert appropriate pictures from Clip Art.

You Can... **Use an interactive whiteboard for sorting and classifying**

Using an interactive whiteboard provides a simple, yet visually stimulating way to sort and classify plants, animals and materials. There are a wealth of images available in Clip Art, or you can use scanned or digital photographs and simple shapes. The Promethean ACTIVprimary software includes a vast array of themed resources within its Resource Library. These images can be displayed on the whiteboard and sorted into Venn or Carroll diagrams, or a branching database using branching database software or the whiteboard software.

Thinking points

● Be clear about the scientific concepts you are teaching and decide upon the most appropriate method of sorting. For example, you could use a Carroll diagram, Venn diagram or a branching database.

● Remember the importance of practical science investigations. The whiteboard should not be used to replace these. Consider how to use the whiteboard effectively alongside a practical science lesson.

● Check whether your whiteboard includes the resources that you need. It might be necessary to search the Internet or provide your own photographic images for particular subject areas, for example, sorting rocks.

Tips, ideas and activities

● Ask the children to come to the board to sort images into sets and then to label the sets accordingly. Encourage them to think of their own sets. Use images of:
  ● living organisms (*Wings/No wings*; *Four legs/Eight legs*)
  ● objects made of different materials (sort by type of material, or *Natural* and *Man-made*)
  ● different foods (*Vegetables*, *Meat*, *Dairy*, or *Healthy* and *Unhealthy*).

● Have a practical lesson sorting materials with magnetic and non-magnetic properties. On the whiteboard, display two sets (*Magnetic* and *Non-magnetic*) and text labels of the different materials. Sort the labels into the two sets as part of the plenary session. Link the activity to the children's practical work and ask them to make some generalisations, for example, *Iron is magnetic but other metals aren't.*

● Prepare a model for a simple branching database. Create a series of yes/no questions around a theme, for example, animal habitats. Hide the whole screen using the Reveal or Screen Shade tools, then gradually show a picture of an animal after each selection: for example, *Does it live under stones? Yes* (reveal a woodlouse). Demonstrate how to carefully frame questions with yes/no answers, for example, *Does it have six legs?* Link the work to a practical investigation if possible.

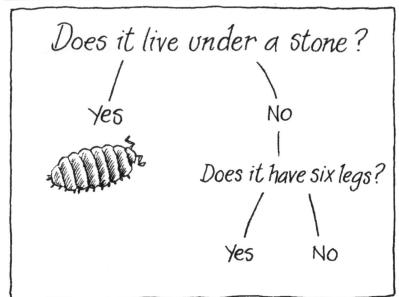

You Can... **Use an interactive whiteboard to investigate sound**

Recording sound is a quick and easy process with the whiteboard. Sound recordings take up little memory and are an ideal, transportable resource for use in a computer suite or with the whole class on the whiteboard PC. All computers come pre-installed with a number of programs that record sound. In order to record, you will need either a webcam or a standard microphone: both options are inexpensive and offer a good standard of quality of sound.

Thinking points

● Consider the flexibility of your classroom set-up. Often the small microphones provided as part of the computer bundle can't pick up noise from further than 1m. If the subject is not within this range, the recording of the investigation might be lost. Also, if the subject cannot move – for example, a large instrument – then you may need to consider using either a PDA or laptop for the sound recording.

● To use the recording facility:

● Click Start and then Programs.

● Next, click Accessories (usually this is found at the top of the My Programs file) and then scroll across to Entertainment.

● Locate the Sound Recorder icon.

● Open the program (it looks like a small grey rectangle with a record button). Place the microphone or web cam as near to the subject as possible (this may be easier using a laptop) and press Record. The program will allow 60 seconds of recording time, which is usually sufficient.

Tips, ideas and activities

● The BBC website offers online resources in sound for nine- to ten-year-olds (www.bbc.co.uk/schools/scienceclips). Online models work best as a stimulus to show how the experiment would work under ideal circumstances (not often found in the primary classroom!). However, they are no substitute to actually doing the experiment. Remember to check copyright restrictions before using images from websites.

● Save your files and store them, so that you reuse the sounds you have recorded.

● The Sound Record program automatically displays the sound waves from the recording. This may not be part of your teaching objective but it offers a worthwhile teaching point. Use this facility for investigations on 'pitch' – playing and recording a range of musical instruments. Play back the sounds to the whole class on the whiteboard and encourage each child to describe the pitch or volume of each instrument using appropriate vocabulary.

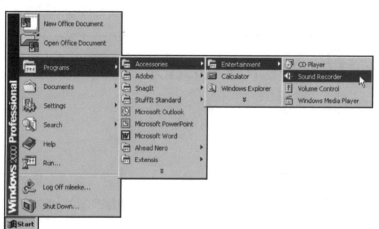

Screenshots reprinted by permission of Microsoft Corporation

● Another use is to record children's comments on investigations for review and assessment purposes. Children in particular find recordings a useful tool for evaluation of work they have done.

You Can... **Use an interactive whiteboard to display and label scientific images**

A whiteboard is a great way to store and display pictures of materials, plants and animals for a variety of purposes. You can use Clip Art, the resources provided with your whiteboard software, images from websites and published books, digital or scanned photographs, or drawings made by you or the children. The pictures can be downloaded or scanned, and then saved on file without any fear of them being lost or damaged. The images can be easily accessed, displayed and manipulated using the whiteboard.

Thinking points

● Always check any copyright restrictions when downloading images from the Internet or scanning pictures from books. The BBC schools website (www.bbc.co.uk/schools/ scienceclips) has some excellent activities on the subject of plants and animals.

● When preparing a lesson using multiple images or flipchart pages, add an extra slide or page at the beginning and type in the lesson objective. This can be referred back to at the end of the lesson with the question: *What have we learned today?*

● A bank of text and images can be made for every year group, gradually adding more details and probing questions to provide progression through the school.

● The same slide show can be referred to several times during the science topic and used as a revision aid. Some slides might also be printed and used as worksheets.

Tips, ideas and activities

● Use PowerPoint to create labelled pictures of plants and animals:

1) Download your chosen image by right-clicking on it. Then click Save As, giving the picture an appropriate name. Alternatively, draw a picture yourself or ask the children to draw one. Scan and save the images into the computer.

2) Open a new PowerPoint presentation. Click Insert, then Picture, then go to From File and find the saved picture. Insert the picture and move it into position. Enlarge it to fill most of the slide.

3) Insert a text box and type in text for the label. Highlight the word with your mouse and select an appropriate font size and style. Move the label into position, slightly away from the stem.

4) Add an arrow from the Drawing Toolbar or from AutoShapes. Click on the arrow icon and select an appropriate arrow. Move the arrow into position. Repeat for each label and arrow.

● Animate labels so that they arrive on a click:
1) Click on the label you want to animate. Click Slide Show, then Custom Animation, add effect entrance and select an appropriate entrance, random effects is usually quite fun.

2) Animate the arrows in the same way. Alternatively, leave them as prompts: ask children what they think each part is called and then reveal the answer with a click.

You Can... **Use an interactive whiteboard to demonstrate forces**

It has always been possible to demonstrate forces in a lively and interactive way. Taking children outside to push and pull scooters and bikes, and exploring forces within the classroom, gives a real feel for force and subsequent movement. With a whiteboard, however, you can demonstrate pushes and pulls on a wider range of objects, many of which are not accessible for practical work.

Thinking points

● There is no substitute for hands on experience. Children need to experience pushing and pulling objects themselves, on a variety of surfaces and slopes.

● Explain to children why it is dangerous to try to stop some moving objects. Extend the discussion to road safety using a video or a CD-ROM, which can be played through the interactive whiteboard.

● Consider how you will use the whiteboard to demonstrate forces – either using a PowerPoint presentation or video resources. Will you use it to introduce concepts before moving to more practical work? Or as a way of reviewing forces, asking individual children to highlight or write on the board key vocabulary or concepts?

Tips, ideas and activities

● There are some excellent activities on the BBC schools website (www.bbc.co.uk/schools/scienceclips/) that work well on a whiteboard, subject to copyright restrictions. The children are asked to make predictions about what they think will happen. The whole class can then try out the virtual experiment and test their predictions.

● Prepare your own PowerPoint presentation to review children's understanding of forces. The presentation will allow you to show objects and forces that are not easily accessible for the purposes of a practical demonstration. Follow the step-by-step instructions below:

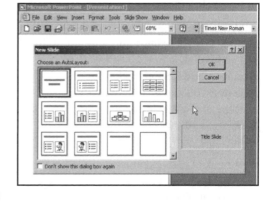

1) Open a blank presentation in Microsoft PowerPoint; select Blank Slide; select Title Slide.

2) Select and insert a title slide into the presentation. Type the objective of the lesson, for example, *To learn about types of forces.*

3) Insert a new Blank Slide.

4) Insert a picture of an object that requires a force to make it move, for example, a car or bus. To do this, find the menu bar, go to Insert, then Picture, and select the Clip Art option. Within Clip Art, the 'Transportation' category will provide you with some suitable images. Close the Insert Clip Art screen.

5) Animate the picture to show how forces work. The object will need to move in the correct direction when the mouse is clicked. There are two ways of doing this, depending which version of PowerPoint you have.

a. If you have PowerPoint 2003: click on the picture so that handles appear around it. Go to Slide Show and then Custom Animation. Click on the Effects tab and select Exit, and then Fly Out. Select 'to right' on the Direction menu, and 'slow' on the Speed menu.

b. If you have earlier versions of PowerPoint, you will have to insert two buses or cars on each slide – one ranged left and one ranged right. Go to Slide Show, then Custom Animation. Check Picture Frame 1 and 2 and make sure that Picture Frame 1 (on the left of the screen) appears first in the Animation order box. Click on the Effects tab. For both pictures, select Fly, then 'from left'. Click on the Preview Animation button. The bus on the left of the screen should appear on the left of the screen, followed by the bus on the right after a mouse click.

c. Add directional arrows. To do this, go to the Drawing toolbar and select AutoShapes and Block Arrows. Select an arrow. The arrow should then appear in your presentation.

6) Click Slide Show and View Show to present your pre-prepared slide show to the children. Ask them in which direction they think the bus will move. Click the mouse and the bus will move to the right.

7) Ask children about other forces acting on the bus. *In which direction will friction act? How can the weight of the bus be shown?* Show the direction of each force, either by using the Pen tool or by inserting text labels.

● Extend the presentation by adding a new slide featuring another object that requires a force to make it to move, for example, a lawnmower, a vacuum cleaner, a tug-of-war rope or a wheelbarrow.

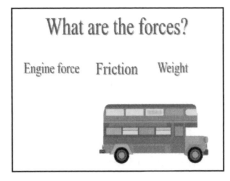

● Collect some suitable pictures from Clip Art (see point number 4 above for instructions). Insert each picture on a separate slide and number them. In Slide Show mode, display each image on the screen in turn. Ask the children to write down the object, its related force and the direction in which the force makes the object move.

● Prepare each picture in PowerPoint, with arrows to represent each force. Hide the arrows and ask children to predict how the forces work on each object. Reveal the arrows at the end of the lesson (see point 5c above for instructions).

You Can... **Use an interactive whiteboard with a digital microscope**

A digital microscope was sent to every school as part of Science Year 2002, so this resource should be available to you. Children are fascinated by microscopes. The interactive whiteboard affords an opportunity to engage the whole class in an experience that makes everyone feel like a 'real' scientist. As well as developing observations skills, widening children's knowledge of real applications of ICT and allowing them to see things in a whole new light, working with a digital microscope is also great fun! Children can also be encouraged to feed back to the class using the microscope and whiteboard, to develop skills in speaking and listening.

Thinking points

● If you haven't used the microscope before, spend time exploring its functions and software before presenting it to the class.

● Choose a couple of ICT 'whizz-kids' (every class has them) and allow them time to 'play' with the microscope. They will soon become experts and will be invaluable assistants to you later.

● The Intel microscope (Intel QX3+) can be used in its cradle – like a traditional microscope – or hand-held as a camera. Practise using it in both ways.

● When you place a sample on a slide beneath the microscope, a large image will be projected on to the whiteboard. Be careful when changing the focus on the microscope, as it can take a moment for the computer to catch up.

● The microscope may be used as a camera and a movie-maker and enables time-lapse photography, which provides excellent opportunities for scientific investigation and some obvious links to literacy and numeracy.

Tips, ideas and activities

● Grow yeast in petri dishes. The children will be spellbound as they watch the microbes grow. The activity will also extend their knowledge of variables in experiments.

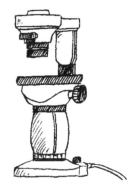

● Look at different surfaces using the microscope in hand-held mode. Compare and describe their relative roughness and explain how this affects the amount of friction.

● Model comparing and classifying rocks, sharing the techniques and vocabulary needed to describe and identify them. Examine soils of different qualities in a similar way.

● Study a tooth, looking at its structure and observing the effects of decay when it is dropped in a fizzy drink. Test different types of drink.

● Support understanding of the functions of plant parts, by looking at roots, stems, leaves and flowers under the microscope. Reproduction in plants is a difficult concept and involves much new vocabulary. Also, real flowers never look like the diagrams used to explain pollination and fertilisation!

● Magnify the insides of real flowers. Take pictures of samples, label them and use the images in a report.

● Use the 'movie-maker' function of the microscope to classify, observe and record the behaviour of minibeasts. Investigate the conditions woodlice prefer, for example, or which leaves aphids like to eat.

You Can... Use an interactive whiteboard to investigate how our bodies work

Models on an interactive whiteboard are a great way of showing what goes on inside the human body. The images are larger and clearer than any poster, and in many cases actually show the body part in action, for example blood flowing round the body. Connecting a digital microscope to your computer can also help you to produce some interesting images to form part of a discussion or investigation.

Thinking points

● Consider whether your room is dark enough for the class to see the fine detail of a full-screen image of the body. Drawing blinds may help to get the maximum effect from the data projector. The screen background can also be varied to enhance the screen images. Alternatively, consider purchasing a projector with a higher lumen count (this refers to the brightness of the projector).

● Research the various resources that are available, through Clip Art, published materials and websites. Visual models, for example of a beating heart or a child growing in the womb, are extremely effective when shown on the interactive whiteboard and can be used as a dramatic introduction to your lesson.

● Consider ways of using your digital microscope when studying the human body, and make sure the microscope is easily accessible for use with the whiteboard.

Tips, ideas and activities

● The web site www.bbc.co.uk/science/humanbody provides an interactive human body. Children can drag and drop organs, muscles and skeleton body parts on to the human frame. This provides a useful visual overview of the human body and illustrates where all the body parts are situated, although the activities are not necessarily intended for children.

● Use a model of the human skeleton (from Clip Art, or from the whiteboard's Gallery or Resources Library) to challenge children to drag and drop labels such as *ribs*, *spine* and *skull*, or to make observations and annotate different features of the skeleton.

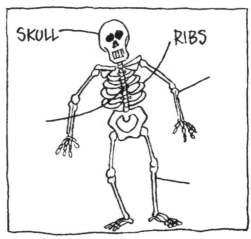

● Collect information, using Microsoft Excel, that can be used by children to quickly produce graphs and charts (for example, the heights of the children in the class). These can then be projected on to the whiteboard.

● Connect a digital microscope to the whiteboard to study, in great detail, parts of the anatomy.

● Photograph a number of images from the body (skin, hair, eyelash, tongue) with the digital microscope and invite the children to guess what the images are and to describe the purpose of that part of the body.

You Can... Use an interactive whiteboard with a datalogger

An electronic datalogger can be used to collect changing information on temperature, sound or light. At the end of the investigation period, the logger can then be linked to a computer and graphs of the data held quickly displayed. The advantage of using a datalogger with a whiteboard is that graphs showing the collected data can be easily displayed and annotated so that children can see and interpret data in groups or as a whole class.

Thinking points

● Using a datalogger provides much more accurate measurements than using analogue devices.

● Devices can be set up so that they will log data on change in light, sound or temperature over a period of up to 24 hours.

● Graphs can be produced both very quickly and accurately and once displayed on the whiteboard this allows much more time for analysis and interpretation of what the data is actually showing.

● Look out for changing scales on the graphs once the data is displayed, especially if you are using two dataloggers to compare any information collected.

● The section right shows you how to set up one activity using dataloggers. Consider how this activity could be adapted and how dataloggers could be used for other aspects of science work.

Tips, ideas and activities

● Set up two dataloggers to record changing temperatures. Place one inside the classroom and one outside. Set them to record over a period of time; 24 hours should be sufficient.

● Enter the two sets of data into the computer and create a line graph for each one. Label each graph to avoid confusion.

● Repeat the process, recording changing light and sound over time.

● Discuss the temperature data using the whiteboard. Before showing the children any data, ask them to predict: *Which logger do you think will show the highest temperature? What do you think will happen to the graph displaying data from the outside logger at midnight? At daybreak?*

● Display the temperature data and graphs. Ask the children to describe any difference between the data logged inside the classroom and that logged outside.

● Ask the children to highlight or annotate any steep rises or falls in the graphs and to tell you at what times these happen. Ask why they think the graphs change at these times.

● Repeat using the light graphs and then the sound graphs.

● Show the data from all three graphs plotted together, one showing outside data, and one showing inside data. Ask the children to tell you how the graphs for temperature, light and sound are different and whether they show what they would have expected.

You Can... **Use an interactive whiteboard to investigate materials**

The whiteboard can be used effectively to sort materials and classify their properties. Displays of materials can be created, with which children can then interact. This section gives suggestions to create your own presentations focusing on the properties of materials. Alternatively you may prefer to use a presentation downloaded from a website, or from a CD-ROM. Don't forget that there is no substitute for direct hands-on experience. The whiteboard should be used to enhance and reinforce the children's learning about materials.

Thinking points

● Children need to experience feeling and manipulating different materials, as well as viewing them on the whiteboard. It is only through hands-on experience that children will learn to describe materials using the correct vocabulary.

● Consider how you will use the whiteboard to investigate materials. Will you use the whiteboard to introduce concepts before moving to more practical work? Or will you use it as a way of reviewing work on materials, with individual children highlighting, or writing on the board, key vocabulary or concepts?

● There are many good CD-ROMs available that provide interactive activities for sorting and classifying materials. The BBC website (www.bbc.co.uk/schools/scienceclips/) also has some activities which work well on a whiteboard, subject to copyright restrictions. Children are asked to sort materials, or make predictions about what will happen when materials are heated or immersed in water. The whole class can try out the experiment on the whiteboard and test their predictions.

Tips, ideas and activities

● Display an image showing a range of different materials, for example a window with a wooden frame and curtains, or a picture of a car with door open showing both the inside and outside. Ask children to highlight different materials and to identify them.

● List different materials in text boxes on the left-hand side of the slide: for example, glass, metal, wood. List a range of properties of materials in text boxes on the right hand side: for example, *will attract a magnet, is waterproof*. Ask children to link each material to a property using the Arrow or Pen tools.

● Vary the above activity by challenging older children to identify all the properties associated with each material.

● Create a similar activity to the one above, listing materials on one side to what happens on contact with heat or water on the other side.

● Collect a range of pictures, put them all on to one slide and number them. Display the pictures and ask the children to list the properties of each material in their books. This activity is good for assessment and for reinforcing the correct scientific language.

● Save any presentations you have prepared for use at another time, or for revision.

You Can... **Use an interactive whiteboard with a webcam**

Webcams have been around for several years but they are only now coming into their own as a useful resource in the classroom. Although webcams are not a standard attachment to the interactive whiteboard, they are very simple to install. They have only a very basic pixel ratio but they are nevertheless ideal for sharing or 'web conferencing' scientific investigations.

Thinking points

● Webcams are designed as a low-end filming tool, so neither the sound nor the picture quality is of a particularly high standard. However, if you are willing to accept this, it is possible to create some interesting and interactive lessons using the webcam.

● Webcams can be used for web conferencing which is in its infancy. The larger messaging groups (Yahoo and Microsoft Network) offer video conferencing alongside their instant messaging and email communications.

● Check that your school's firewall will not prevent you from connecting with another user. Contact your technician for further support.

● Sound echoes may mean that your echo settings are too high. Look in the View folder to change these settings. If there is feedback, move the speakers away from the microphone. Feedback can be eliminated by using a microphone headset, though this can only be used by one person at a time.

Tips, ideas and activities

● To use the webcam:

1) Access your webcam either in the bottom right-hand corner of the Toolbar or in My Computer. Find the correct drive and double click it – it will usually display a camera or video recorder to represent the webcam.

2) Focus the webcam on the object you wish to film. Set the camera to take a photograph at regular intervals, such as every two hours.

3) Display the resulting photographs on the whiteboard.

● Photographs taken with the webcam can be linked to practical work on reversible and irreversible changes or changing states. For example, use the webcam to monitor a strawberry decaying over two days.

● Photographs taken with the webcam can be linked to work on data collection. For example, use the webcam to observe the different species that visit the school bird table, and ask the children to keep a record.

● Use the webcam as a conference tool with another class or school. The number of frames per second that can be generated will be reliant on the speed of your Internet connection. If your school is using broadband, the camera will run at around 20–30 frames per second. This will produce a video-like image, though there is often a sound delay!

You Can... **Use an interactive whiteboard to examine historical sources of evidence**

A whiteboard enables sources of evidence to be displayed as large colour images on the screen, so that the whole class can discuss their findings together. Using the whiteboard provides an exciting opportunity to access new sources of evidence. Many older resources can be revamped, and a scanner is invaluable for importing favourite pictures or texts (subject to copyright). A link to the Internet also offers access to a wealth of primary evidence. Images can easily be saved for later use without copies becoming frayed at the edges.

Thinking points

● Expose children to as many sources of evidence as possible. This will develop an enquiry-based approach and an appreciation of the uses of ICT for secondary research.

● Explore the increasing number of electronic big books dedicated to QCA units of work for History, many of which are rich in images and quality text.

● Collect small artefacts, like coins, jewellery, stamps or medals. Share them with the whole class using the whiteboard. Take digital photos of the artefacts. Alternatively, place the artefact on the viewing tray of a digital microscope and a large image will be projected onto the whiteboard.

● Think about how you will use each resource. The whiteboard gives you the opportunity to Highlight (or Spotlight) features of a text or image, to organise them into a presentation, to resize for ease of use, or to annotate in order to pick out key points linked to your objectives.

Tips, ideas and activities

● Take photographs of recent historical evidence in the locality, for example, old buildings and gravestones. Display them as a slideshow on the whiteboard. Alternatively, create a poster using your whiteboard software. Link it to separate flipchart pages asking questions about each object.

● Ask children to bring in old photos of family members or special occasions. Display them on the whiteboard. Discuss what each image shows and what evidence it presents about how people used to live.

● Create a slideshow or PowerPoint presentation on Ancient Greek or Roman buildings. Images can be obtained from the Internet (subject to copyright restrictions), for example, www.thebritishmuseum.ac.uk/education. Study the construction and purpose of buildings.

● Display a picture of an obscure tool or artefact from the period studied. Ask children to describe it. Speculate on its origins and purposes.

● Create a database from census materials showing information on former residents of the area. Ask children to comment on the size of families, extended families living together, longevity, immigration patterns and unusual occupations.

● Download newsreels from www.britishpathe.com. These provide an excellent source of primary evidence. Show clips of historical scenes or events, copyright permitting.

You Can... **Use an interactive whiteboard to empathise with people from the past**

Children often regard the past as unimportant because they perceive that people and events from earlier times don't affect them. Sources of evidence often tell us the 'what, when, where and who', but seldom inform us about peoples emotional responses. The whiteboard can become a 'window' to the past, developing children's understanding of and empathy with people from long ago.

Thinking points

● Historical photographs available to buy in packs can be copied from books or the Internet (copyright permitting). Well-chosen, they can help generate discussion on the lives of people from the past. Extend such discussions into drama or creative writing activities.

● Play sound archives on the Internet to the class through the whiteboard. Play excerpts from historical films and documentaries. Check that your whiteboard PC includes a DVD software player (such as Cyberlink PowerDVD Player).

● Display extracts from accounts of historical events and lives from the past. Fictional narratives such as *Carrie's War* by Nina Bawden (Puffin Books) can provide insights into conditions experienced by people from the past. Contemporary non-fiction texts may also be used for this purpose, for example Samuel Pepys' diary or quotes from Lord Shaftsbury's reports on factories.

Tips, ideas and activities

● Scan (or copy) photographs and present them as slide shows or insert them into programs like PowerPoint, providing a large, bold and vivid focus for the whole class.

● Scan (or copy) text extract, copyright permitting. During shared reading, highlight emotive descriptions or imagery on the whiteboard.

● Create a piece of collaborative writing to help children understand people's situations from different perspectives.

● Copy works of art from the Internet into PowerPoint (subject to copyright restrictions), to provide a stimulus for enquiry about conditions in different periods. Study characters from paintings and ask children to build up a profile from the visual information.

● Download newsreels showing historical events and periods from www.britishpathe.com, and watch them on the whiteboard. Highlight a particular person using the Pen tool and freeze-frame, or use the Screen Capture facility. Ask children to imagine the feelings and thoughts of that individual.

● Show suitable excerpts from films set in different historical periods. Make sure children are aware these were filmed after the periods studied and should be treated cautiously as secondary sources of evidence, since historians may not have advised the film makers. Documentaries offer a more authoritative secondary source.

● Visit the BBC historical websites for Key Stage 2. Work through the activities as a class and use as a stimulus for drama work, hot seating or freeze-frames.

You Can... **Use an interactive whiteboard to investigate the local area**

Using photographs taken by a digital camera can provide a quick way of identifying key characteristics in your local area. By downloading the shots onto your whiteboard, you can examine these characteristics closely as a whole class and enlarge aspects in a way that beats any photocopier!

Thinking points

● Children need training in using a digital camera. Although it may be useful to have a small trained 'team' of children who are experts at downloading and using the photographs and the cameras, they, in turn, should act as peer group teachers to others.

● Check whether the school or LEA have a policy for lending out digital cameras.

● If digital cameras are not available, many websites have aerial photographs and maps available to download.

● More whiteboard companies are now including simple map-making tools as part of their standard package. If your whiteboard software includes one of these tools, explore its potential application in your locality project.

Tips, ideas and activities

● Loan a digital camera to each child in turn to take photographs of important features of their street or local area. In school, copy and paste the photographs into a document as part of a locality exercise. Save the documents on to a diskette or memory stick and transfer them to the interactive whiteboard so that the class can share each other's work – perhaps in the form of an *Our local area* PowerPoint presentation, or an interactive poster with links from each of the photographs to information about them.

● Take photographs of key landmarks and streets and use images taken from local history websites to compare and contrast your photographs with images from the same locations taken in the past.

● Use the Drawing or Pen tools to label and highlight features when working with photographs on the whiteboard. Invite the children to add their own comments or annotations.

● Link with a school in a different county, or even country. Email photographs from your local area and ask your partner school to do the same. Use the photographs to compare and contrast another area with the children's own locality.

● Visit a website, such as www.multimap.co.uk, that shows the school both as an aerial map and in standard OS format.

You Can... Use an interactive whiteboard to see the world

The term World Wide Web clearly suggests the wide reach of the Internet and the wealth of resources it can access. From tourist websites to radio and television news sites, it is possible to view information and images from any country in the world. Indeed the NASA website allows the user not only to see this world, but also Mars and other planets. With a webcam in class, moreover, it is not only possible to see the world but to interact with it in return.

Thinking points

● Check that your interactive whiteboard computer has access to the Internet. If it doesn't it would be worth investing in it; without an Internet connection, you and your colleagues will only be able to access a very small proportion of the whiteboard's capabilities, particularly when studying other countries and cultures around the world.

● Consider which aspect of a country's culture is being studied. It is quite easy to be overwhelmed by web information. Define your search criteria and use search engines, such as www.google.co.uk or www.yahoo.co.uk to find the information you are looking for.

● Check whether your school or LEA have an international link or 'twinning' partnership. If so, investigate how you can develop the links between children through email, digital photo swaps, webcam video links or file sharing.

Tips, ideas and activities

● If you are looking for an image – for example, a map or flag – these can be filtered out of searches by clicking on the 'Image only' button (usually located next to the search box). The search will then only locate images from websites, rather than the websites themselves.

● If you are focusing on one country, most states and countries have good interactive tourist information websites. These websites usually include geographical information – climate, population density, main exports and imports – and often have information on local news and events as well.

● Most local television or radio stations now have websites. The quality is variable but radio stations in particular can be a great source of local news, music and culture.

● Many towns and tourist information sites have webcams attached to places of local interest.

● Weather sites (for example, www.bbc.co.uk/weather) often show five-day forecasts from anywhere in the world. It is very interesting to compare the weather in Tobago, for example, with the United Kingdom and there are many potential curriculum links that can arise from this activity, such as finding differences, real-life applications of negative numbers, data handling, and so on. All of these can be introduced through the medium of the whiteboard.

You Can... Use an interactive whiteboard to illustrate processes in design and technology

The creation of a product is the result of a process: research, the formation of ideas, design, testing and evaluating, and manufacture. Increasingly, technology is supporting children in this process. A whiteboard can be used to bring a visual element to the design process. It is also useful in helping children form and communicate their ideas, learn how to work with tools and to effectively evaluate the work of others.

Thinking points

● Consider using the whiteboard to reinforce the sequence of an activity, or its safety implications. Having a list of steps, or a dos and don'ts list on the board can serve as a visual reminder, particularly with children who find it difficult to remember instructions.

● Consider the use of other equipment to help the children see the design process. A digital video camera, when attached to the whiteboard, can help children to clearly see a teacher demonstration. This is especially useful when designing or making a complex or detailed product.

● Encourage the children to use the Internet to search and gather information to develop their ideas and plan their project. For example, older children set with the task of designing a slipper could research the design and construction of different types of footwear. Younger children planning to build a toy car could be encouraged to research different types of vehicles.

Tips, ideas and activities

● Generate ideas for a design using drawing or graphics software. Ask children to annotate them, to refine or improve the design. Drawings can be rendered using representations of the correct materials or textures, to give a realistic impression of the finished product.

● Ask children to identify the risks of using saws and other tools and display their suggestions. They are more likely to remember the risks if they have been involved in identifying them.

● Insert a digital image of a tool, then ask the children to add instructions detailing how to use it safely. For younger children, a symbol could be used instead of text.

● Most boards have a selection of transparent tools, and some include measuring tools such as rulers and protractors. Use these to demonstrate how to measure accurately, for example by drawing a lightly-coloured rectangular shape and placing the ruler over it. When the children are making picture frames, use the protractor to demonstrate how a mitred joint is made.

● Take digital photographs of the children's completed products. In the next lesson, encourage the children to respond to these and to evaluate them. Ask questions such as: *Which products do you like the best? Why? How could the work be improved?*

You Can... Use an interactive whiteboard to improve children's performance in PE

PE lessons encourage active participation, and also encompass other elements such as performance, strategy, skills practice and the process of review and evaluation. The use of a whiteboard is particularly useful for the evaluation of children's performance in PE. You can use digital photography and video or film clips for this purpose. However, ICT can also be used for a range of related activities, for example, knowledge and understanding of fitness and health.

Thinking points

● If you use the whiteboard for PE, allot small amounts of time for this during the day. This will ensure that time allocated for practical work is not consumed. Ideally, these time slots should be just before a break, or just after the children have settled down following quiet reading.

● Consider using photographs, and digital video taken during PE lessons, to inform your planning and assessment. This type of evidence can be invaluable as a mental and visual reminder when you are writing reports.

● Think carefully about how the photographs or video clips could be used to illustrate your teaching points. Decide upon your focus in advance, for example, style, balance, teamwork or fluency of movement.

● Think about how you will encourage the children to evaluate their work. A balance shown on a slide, for example, could be annotated with a thick whiteboard pen to show the correct position.

● Subject to copyright, explore the use of video clips from dance companies depicting dances from different times, places and cultures.

Tips, ideas and activities

● During a lesson on different types of balances, use a digital camera to take pictures of each balance, Take pictures of good single and paired balances, as well as balances which could be improved. Display these on the whiteboard and ask the children to evaluate them. Ask open-ended questions to encourage children to extend their answers. The Primary National Strategy's *Learning and Teaching Using ICT* (2004) includes specific activities for reviewing children's performance in PE using the interactive whiteboard. This includes lesson plans, pupil activities and video clips.

● Take five digital photographs of different gymnastic movements. Display these on a flipchart, in a random order. Ask the children to perform the movements in the pictures, one after the other. When they have finished, ask one child to arrange the images in a different order. Ask the class to perform the new routine on the board. *Which routine was better? Why?*

● Use ICT for a range of activities related to PE, for example, athletics, orienteering, and knowledge and understanding of fitness and health. Use heart monitors to measure heart beats during a race, or navigate around a course using a Roamer. Respond to the evidence provided by these activities in the classroom, using the whiteboard.

You Can... **Use an interactive whiteboard to create variations on a musical composition**

Music composition programs are ideally suited for the interactive whiteboard. Such programs are often similar to computer games where musical notation or icons are dragged and dropped into a frame on the screen. Some packages, such as Compose World Junior *(ESP software), are loaded with hundreds of musical phrases that, when put together, can create a range of songs. On an interactive whiteboard, with the speakers plugged in, they look and sound good and are fun to use.*

Thinking points

● Think about your musical objective. Ensure that the composition program that you are using fits the objectives you are covering. There are several composition programs available that have excellent production values, but do not necessarily have appropriate applications in the classroom.

● Check that you will be able to save the work when it is completed. Many programs do not allow the user to save their work. If this is the case, ask children to note down or print out their final musical arrangements so they can reproduce them. Alternatively, screen shots can be taken and displayed on the whiteboard for review.

● Consider how the children will listen to their music while composing it. In a computer suite, headphones are an essential requirement. However, finished pieces can be displayed on the interactive whiteboard for the whole class to see and hear.

● Check the Gallery or Resources library in your whiteboard, which may provide very useful software for the creation of musical compositions.

Tips, ideas and activities

● There are many very useful resources available in the 'music room' at www.bbc.co.uk/schools/communities/onionstreet. This site provides a range of musical themes, the potential to download a mixer and links to many resources from across the world to enable children to create their own music.

● This type of work links closely to the QCA Scheme of Work for IT, Unit 3c *Manipulating sound*. Plan a project linking ICT to music. The children, in groups, can compose a piece of music using composition software (or actual instruments). They can then prepare a PowerPoint presentation, with images that match the mood of the piece. This can be presented to, and reviewed by, the whole class using the whiteboard. The benefit of using composition software is that the pieces can be organised and reorganised as required.

● Create a set of musical cards on the whiteboard. Prepare some Clip Art images of musical instruments with their associated sounds. Ask the children to identify each instrument's sound, and describe its timbre (or quality).

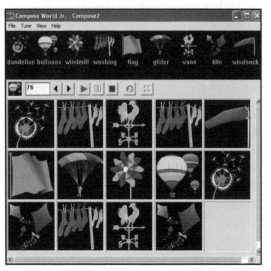

From Compose World Junior, ESP software

You Can... Use an interactive whiteboard to examine works of art

Exploring the work of artists is a visual task and the whiteboard is an excellent tool for whole-class teaching of art appreciation, deconstruction and techniques. The interactive whiteboard brings art to life, as images, artefacts and sculptures can be shared in detail with the whole class. Images can be found on the Internet, or scanned in from books or postcards (but remember that it is important to check any copyright restrictions before copying or manipulating such images). The whiteboard can become both an art gallery and a workshop all in one!

Thinking points

● Make sure the images you plan to show are of a good quality. In particular, ensure images obtained from the Internet are still clear when enlarged.

● Images displayed on the whiteboard can be large and vivid. Choose pictures with strong colours to demonstrate the effect of colour on mood.

● Use search engines on the Internet to find images (for example, www.google.co.uk or www.askjeeves.co.uk). Save useful sites in Favourites, so that it is easy to find more images when they are needed. Remember to check copyright restrictions before using images from websites.

● Most schools have a wealth of artwork of different types, though many are too small for whole-class teaching. Scan these into the PC and save them in My Pictures. Annotating, drawing on or highlighting elements of compositions can enhance children's understanding of art. (Again, remember to check copyright restrictions.) Consider running pictures as a slideshow, to help draw out the focus of the lesson.

Tips, ideas and activities

● Display works by similar artists and analyse them to develop children's understanding of artistic style. Explain methods and composition. Conversely, compare paintings of different styles but with similar subjects.

● Demonstrate how to search multimedia encyclopaedias and the Internet for images, or information on artists or styles. Art galleries and museums often have interactive sites.

● Display a landscape painting to develop understanding of depth. Label foreground, middle ground and background using the Pen tool.

● Illustrate perspective by first identifying elements of a composition that recede into the distance (trees, lamp posts and roads for example) and discussing their relative size and position. Next, draw over these with coloured pen to emphasise how their size diminishes with distance.

● Display images of paintings, artefacts or sculptures from the same period. Ask children to write descriptive reports or narratives based on observation.

● Display digital photos of children's work in progress and annotate elements for discussion. Analysing children's artwork celebrates success, provides a model for others and develops critical responses.

● Take a digital photograph of a child. Display it on the whiteboard for children to practise sketching the human form. In this way, the child who is the model can participate in the sketching too.

You Can... Use an interactive whiteboard to investigate colour and texture

There are many paint packages available for ICT. Children enjoy using such packages and they help to develop their artistic understanding. Demonstrating the use of paint packages on the whiteboard not only shows how these programs can be used, but also illustrates to children how creative and inspiring digital art can be. If you do not have any paint software, use the palette available on Microsoft Word to investigate colour. For example, you can create different coloured squares and arrange them next to each other in different combinations as a basis for discussion about colour.

Thinking points

● Some degree of colour blindness is not uncommon. Be aware that one or two children may not be able to easily distinguish between all shades. Consider changing backgrounds (see right) to make a painting or image accessible to all.

● The whiteboard is a great help when looking at colour and texture but is not a substitute for the real experience of creating their own collages and paintings. Use the whiteboard to introduce children to different techniques and processes and to review their work at the end of a lesson.

● Paint packages offer a wealth of different tools, many of which are also available on whiteboard software, for example the Spray tool to demonstrate colour and light, or the Fill tool to create visual effects. Make sure you understand how to use each tool and the potential applications of each one.

Tips, ideas and activities

● Some paint packages allow colour mixing. Ask children to predict, for example, what happens when blue and yellow are mixed.

● Display a small part of a painting and ask children to describe the colours they can see.

● Ask children what colours or shades they would use to paint a sky. Display just the sky from a well-known painting (for example, Van Gogh's *A Cornfield with Cypresses*). Examine it closely, to show children the many different colours that have been used.

● Check the readability of different coloured text against different coloured backgrounds. Discuss various colour combinations with the children: *Which are easy to read and which are difficult?*

● Change the texture on digital photographs using a paint package. For example, make the brick of the school building furry, or give plants a metallic look.

● Scan in children's painted pictures and display them on the whiteboard. Ask the rest of the class what colours and colour mixes have been used to create the paintings. Then ask the artists themselves.

● Combine the children's work and ask each child to add text to describe each picture. Use this as the basis for a multimedia presentation and exchange it with other classes for feedback and review.

You Can... **Use an interactive whiteboard to show and compare places of worship**

It has always been a challenge to get hold of appropriate religious artefacts and pictures for whole-class work. With a whiteboard and the Internet, these resources can be accessed easily and cheaply, and can be enlarged so that they are accessible to all. Many children will have little or no experience of religious artefacts or buildings, so resources such as these are very useful.

Thinking points

● Collect suitable pictures of religious buildings. If you live near different places of worship, ask for permission to photograph them. Learning will be reinforced by the proximity of these buildings to where the children live. If it is not possible to take photos, then search the Internet for suitable pictures or use Clip Art images.

● Remember to save your photographs. They can then be accessed at any time and for different purposes.

● Always check copyright when downloading, scanning or in any way manipulating pictures.

● There is no substitute for a visit to a local place of worship. Schools are made very welcome and it is a memorable experience for the pupils. Use the whiteboard to introduce the idea of the visit, and to review children's experiences of it.

Tips, ideas and activities

● Use the images of religious buildings that you have collected and saved to create a PowerPoint presentation. Click Insert and find the picture icon. Search for your saved picture and click Insert again. The picture will appear in the slide. Give the picture a title.

● Add a title slide detailing the objective of the lesson. Add slides before and after each of the picture slides and use these to ask key questions. When you play the presentation to the children, discuss each slide in turn. Return to the title slide at the end of the lesson to review what the children have learned.

● Alternatively, encourage groups of children to put together the presentations. Ask them to draw out similarities and differences between the different religious buildings and to write these on the board, or to annotate the pictures using the Pen or Highlighter tools.

● Encourage the children to prepare a 'script' for their presentation, and to decide who will deliver it. Allow them time to rehearse the presentation and to practise using the whiteboard tools.

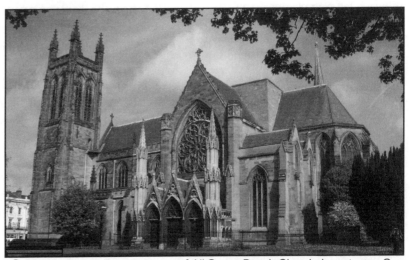

© Scholastic Ltd. By permission of All Saints Parish Church, Leamington Spa.

Whiteboard diary

Teacher's name: _____

Date	Subject/ Objective	How was the whiteboard used?	Evaluation

You Can... **Use an interactive whiteboard** **59**

Whiteboard resources library

Teacher's name: _____

Name of resource and file location	Description of resource	How resource was used	Date resource was used

Lesson planning using the whiteboard

Title of lesson

Objectives
- Be clear about what you want the children to learn.

Prior learning
- Review what children already know, or need to be reminded of before the lesson.

Vocabulary
- Think about the key words children need to recall during the lesson. Should these be displayed on the whiteboard?

How will the whiteboard be used?
- Decide whether to use the whiteboard for the starter, the main teaching activity or the plenary session.

Starter activity
- Decide upon the purpose of the starter.
- Consider whether you will need to refer back to any prior learning or saved files from earlier whiteboard lessons.
- If preparing resources for the whiteboard, decide how long each will take to work through, given the time available for a starter activity.
- Keep a record of any screens used.
- Check copyright restrictions before using images from websites.

Main activity
- Think about the sequence of what you will do and what you want the children to do.
- Prepare the learning resources for the whiteboard before the lesson, including displaying the lesson objectives and using illustrations wherever possible.
- Keep the teaching and learning activities concise, using no more than three or four screens.
- Write down any questions you think you will need to ask the children.
- Plan what children will do for their group or independent learning activities.

Plenary session
- Ask children what they have found out
- Prepare questions to ask the children.
- Decide whether you will ask children to present any of their learning on the whiteboard. If so, allow additional time for them to prepare their materials.
- Think about whether you will need to refer back to any whiteboard resources presented earlier in the lesson.
- Finally, refer back to the learning objectives presented at the start of the lesson to consolidate children's learning.

After the lesson
- Write down the links to schemes of work as well as to the National Curriculum.
- Make a note of any books or websites you may have used.
- Make a quick note of anything you would do differently.
- Save the lesson plan in both a paper and electronic file so that you can find it easily next time.
- You may find it helpful to save whiteboard screens that have been annotated with children's ideas, so that you can adjust your original lesson if you wish to use it again.

Additional Resources

Advice

● Becta, which is responsible to the DfES for ICT in education, provides advice on the use of whiteboards at **www.ictadvice.org.uk.** To access the information you require simply input 'whiteboards' into the search facility on the site.

● Becta also offers advice and guidance for schools thinking of purchasing interactive whiteboards under the 'Interactive whiteboards project'. This section of the site summarises the equipment that is available under the scheme. **www.becta.org.uk/leaders/leaders.cfm?section-3_1&id=3170**

Classroom resources

● The National Whiteboard Network at **www.nwnet.org.uk** provides resources for whiteboard use across the curriculum and advice on accessing whiteboard software. Teachers are also encouraged to add their own resources to the site.

● Whiteboard manufacturers Promethean and SMART Board both provide resources for teaching and learning and case studies of whiteboard use.
weblinks: **www.prometheanworld.com/uk/**
www.smartboard.co.uk/

● There are many free resources available for use with the whiteboard at **www.bbc.co.uk/schools** and **www.standards. dfes.gov.uk/primary/mathematics.** The Standards Site includes a range of free mathematical tools that may be downloaded for use with the whiteboard within the Interactive teaching programs (ITPs).

● EDpaX Ltd have designed a step-by-step program of interactive whiteboard lessons aligned directly to the National Curriculum. Visit **www.edpax.com** for further information

● The Ready Resources series (Scholastic) is a multimedia package which comprises a CD-ROM full of classroom material, and a comprehensive teacher's book of notes. The images, sound, video and text are all specially chosen to match the curriculum and the QCA Schemes of Work. **www.scholastic.co.uk/readyresources**

● Penpals for Handwriting CD-ROM (Cambridge Hitachi), is a resource for teaching handwriting designed for use with an interactive whiteboard. Included are teacher's notes and homework sheets for each unit. Available at **www.cambridge.org**

Additional Resources

- Available from TTS Group Ltd, the QX5 Computer Microscope includes presentation software for slideshows and videos of the children's work on the whiteboard. There is also a companion booklet available separately.
Weblink: **www.tts-group.co.uk**

- The Olympus C-770 is a 3.9 megapixel digital camera which can be used with a whiteboard. It incorporates a 1.8" LCD screen and a 10x optical zoom. See **www.olympus.co.uk**

- Nikon make a 7 megapixel digital camera which will take video with audio. The Coolpix 7900 has a long battery life which can take 220 images, and includes a 2" LCD screen. Visit **www.nikon.co.uk** for further details.

Videos
- To see many and varied examples on video of whiteboards being used across the primary curriculum look out for the Primary National Strategy: *Learning and Teaching Using ICT* resource. This resource consists of a pack of CD-ROMs, for each year including the Foundation Stage and supports the use of ICT and whiteboards across all subjects. The pack was available free to schools in 2004. Contact the DfES Publications Centre at dfes@prolog.uk.com; tel 0845 60 222 60.

Research
- For details of research on interactive whiteboards and case studies of whiteboard practice go to **client.cant.ac.uk/ research/papers**

In this series:

ISBN 0-439-96522-5
ISBN 978-0439-96522-4

You Can:
Create a calm classroom

Noisy classroom?
Stressed children?

Don't worry, You Can: Create a calm classroom offers 50 simply ways to motivate your children and take the stress out of teaching.

ISBN 0-439-96523-3
ISBN 978-0439-96523-1

ISBN 0-439-96534-9
ISBN 978-0439-96534-7

You Can: Survive your early years Ofsted inspection

Don't feel overwhelmed by the onset of an Ofsted inspection - we can help you survive it. This book provides straightforward information and practical advice to support your self-evaluation procedures, whatever the setting, and to achieve a successful Ofsted report.

ISBN 0-439-96539-X
ISBN 978-0439-96539-2

You Can: Use an interactive whiteboard

This easy-to-follow format provides 50 creative tips on how to get to grips with interactive whiteboards and to use them effectively in the classroom. Whether you are a first-time or experienced user, these books offer a wealth of ideas to make the best use of your interactive whiteboard to teach all the curriculum subjects.

ISBN 0-439-96540-3
ISBN 978-0439-96540-8

To find out more, call: 0845 603 9091
or visit our website www.scholastic.co.uk